Memory Palace

The Ultimate Memory
Improvement Technique

(Expand Your Knowledge Base for Enrichment and Fun)

Samuel Almazan

Published By **Elena Holly**

Samuel Almazan

All Rights Reserved

Memory Palace: The Ultimate Memory Improvement Technique (Expand Your Knowledge Base for Enrichment and Fun)

ISBN   978-1-77485-940-7

No part of this guidebook shall be reproduced in any form without permission in writing from the publisher except in the case of brief quotations embodied in critical articles or reviews.

Legal & Disclaimer

The information contained in this ebook is not designed to replace or take the place of any form of medicine or professional medical advice. The information in this ebook has been provided for educational & entertainment purposes only.

The information contained in this book has been compiled from sources deemed reliable, and it is accurate to the best of the Author's knowledge; however, the Author cannot guarantee its accuracy and validity and cannot be held liable for any errors or omissions. Changes are periodically made to this book. You must consult your doctor or get professional medical advice before using any of the suggested remedies, techniques, or information in this book.

Upon using the information contained in this book, you agree to hold harmless the Author from and against any damages, costs, and expenses, including any legal fees potentially resulting from the application of any of the information provided by this guide. This disclaimer applies to any damages or injury caused by the use and application, whether directly or indirectly, of any advice or information presented, whether for breach of contract, tort, negligence, personal injury, criminal intent, or under any other cause of action.

You agree to accept all risks of using the information presented inside this book. You need to consult a professional medical practitioner in order to ensure you are both able and healthy enough to participate in this program.

TABLE OF CONTENTS

Introduction 1

Chapter 1: What Exactly Is The Memory Palace? 3

Chapter 2: The Memory Palace Journey .. 9

Chapter 3: The Brain Food 27

Chapter 4: It Also Helps To Strengthen Memory 37

Chapter 5: The Reasons We Struggle To Recall 43

Chapter 6: The Power Of Beliefs 61

Chapter 7: Filling Your Face With Food For The Best Memory 95

Chapter 8: The Memory Palace 131

Chapter 9: How Discipline Is The Key To Success 161

Chapter 10: What Do You Have The Potential To Accomplish? 176

Introduction

In this guide, we're going to learn techniques called the mind palace, also known as "the memory palace. The technique helps you retain more information than most people. However, that's not all this book will do Many of the books on the market currently teach you how to use the memory palace but do not teach you how to develop an amazing memory in a holistic manner. What I'm trying to teach you is not just how to utilize your memory, but information on how to enhance your diet and lifestyle to increase your memory well.

What I'm trying to teach you in this brief book is how to utilize the memory palace method to keep stories in mind, recall lists, and even remember random facts more effectively. But you'll also learn how to keep name names and recall quotes, and how to make use of your nutrition and supplements to be able to recall more. If you're eager to develop a memory that will amaze everyone around you and even you Let's begin!

Chapter 1: What Exactly Is The Memory Palace?

You're about to be taught more than the most effective memory techniques that are utilized by virtually every memory guru all over the world. You may be familiar with this method from the TV shows "Sherlock" and "leverage". However, you may not think that having a superhuman-like borderline memory is possible. The positive news? It's. As stated by Harvey Mackay "there's no such thing as a bad brain, just one that isn't trained"

Memory palaces are a method that utilizes the physical experience of traveling through places to aid in remembering better. Through this method you'll be able to transform facts such as quotes, quotations, and other things that must be kept in mind into mental representations of them and then put them in your trip through your mind's palace.

The best part is that we're not just looking at one particular type of memory palace.

Instead, we will actually discover a lesser-known technique that is known as "the roman rooms" also! Memory palaces are employed by nearly all of the world's memory experts as well as memory champions. The reason why memory palaces work so well is that, if we want to remember something with without an image, but by using an image, and then attaching an physical location to the items we would like to keep in mind, we are capable of storing data.

The two kinds of memory palaces that we'll examine in this article are the method of travel as well as the Roman room technique. The journey method is in which you imagine yourself going on an excursion that is well-known to you. When you envision going on the same long walk you've been on several times, select one that is familiar to you. the majority of the landmarks. The reason why you're going to be drawn to remembering landmarks is that when you begin to recall things by putting them in our minds palace and the more landmarks you can remember, the more objects you'll be able to recall. Once you've learned the process of traveling in order to remember something, all you need to do is stroll through the landscape in your head and then look at the surroundings.

The second kind of memory palace that you're learning about is called"Roman Room. The roman room isn't an excursion, but an illustration of the space which you're familiar with. The roman room technique instead of thinking about the objects in a certain arrangement, you're going to connect what you'd like to recall with the various objects in the room. As opposed to the travel method it is more like a computer's RAM. It will allow you to be able look wherever you'd like to, and instantly remember unrelated information.

If you're eager to start learning a successful memory method that allows you to recall anything you want read on.

Why should you bother to learn how to use the memory palace?

The first thought that pops into the minds of many people's minds when they consider studying the memories palace is that it feels to be a lot more effort than it's worth! If you're just beginning to learn about the memory palace, it's likely to be slow and, often, it's a challenge to understand how to use it. However, as you begin to learning process and learn how to utilize the method efficiently, you'll begin to feel elated by the progress you're making, and the number of additional items you'll be able to remember.

Learning to use the memory palace is beneficial for everyday life as well as to impress your friends by recollecting many details. It doesn't matter if you're an hotel host or a waiter at the restaurant, or you're a single mother who keeps a the shopping list The memory palace is an effective method of avoiding using pen and paper , or your phone to record lists.

Utilizing the memory palace, some people have been able remember more than 65,000 numbers in an entire row! If you're among the most experienced people in are able to retain the same amount of information, then us and we could easily recall a list of 20-30 or 40 items with ease. Remember that, even though it might seem like to begin with, so did walking, learning to ride a bicycle and learning to drive. But think about what your life might be like if you had not done the work required to acquire these skills!

Does anyone know how to do this?

Anyone can master the technique of memory palace and it doesn't need you to be an expert or to possess a phenomenal spatial memory. If you're blessed with any spatial memory or visual ability whatsoever The memory palace can be an extremely effective technique that can improve your memory by a lot.

How long will it take to master the skill?

in the novel "Moon strolling along with Einstein" The author was a memory expert after practicing this technique for hours every day for the entire year.

To learn how to apply this technique does not have to take anything like this amount of time, according to my experience, if you work on this method for 20 or 30 minutes every day for 30 days , you'll witness a dramatic improvement in the ability of your brain to keep lists and random information.

It's a difficult task at first, but after a few days, this method is going help you save a lot of time and energy , and it will make an immense difference to your life as well. Do not think that it's time wasted, instead think of it as the time you invest in your own development. Once you've got this technique perfected, it's something that you'll be able to keep forever You must put your energy upfront and it will return to you daily.

Chapter 2: The Memory Palace

Journey

The first and most crucial stage of making a memory palace is to develop an accurate plan in your mind of the walk. You'll need to pick a path that you frequently walk and that is full of various landmarks. The more specific landmarks you are able to remember, the greater the number of things you'll be able to recall in the future.

When I first started to practice the memory palace method, I did not actually have a walk I could recall sufficiently in my mind to be able to apply the method! If this is the case for you as well then you may be able to benefit from doing either of the following If you've got an extremely precise and vivid imagination, then you may be able to make a palace or an outdoor walk entirely from scratch. If you're like me and you're not capable of this, it would be useful to explore the exact location over and over repeatedly.

While I was making my memory palace, I took a trip back into my home from childhood (my mom is still there) and took a walk through the house in a slow pace. I chose a route I could walk and that required minimum doubling back I could in order to aid in the process of learning to remember. Then , I walked around the house in a slow pace, taking in all the furniture, and photographs that were displayed on the walls.

Although I looked similar to Howard Hughes, the inventor who lost his mind, this method helped me create an extremely detailed and real-looking mind map after 10 times walking around my home. Make sure to keep the map into your mind this walk, and all of the details will be permanently embedded into your mind prior to with the mental palace. It will help you keep track of things.

An important thing to be aware of when you build your dream castle and exploring it in the near future is that you must create a vivid picture! While walking around my childhood home that is now my "palace" in my head , I would imagine turning up the intensity of the hues. Through making the colors stronger and vivid, the house was much easier to recall and was much more vivid.

Action item: Take your time and think about this right now, then take around 20 minutes and go through a place you've been to repeatedly until you can observe your surroundings in the same way as if you were there (or perhaps even more than that!)

Pro-tip: You're going to want to follow exactly the same way in your mind every time you visit your memory palace. The journey should be vivid and exact is the most important factor to make the most of this experience. The more vivid the journey is, the more easy it will be to recall. Make sure you don't change the route you follow to build your mind's palace! It could cause you to be confused!

The roman room variations

The method of the journey is beneficial in storing lists. The roman room is helpful to remember information that is not ordered. The reason why the roman room can be so helpful in storing lists of ordered items is because in the journey method, you have to move from one location to the next one in a sequence. It's the same as going all through the alphabet you are unable to find out the seven letters prior to Q without thinking for a moment, and you aren't able to figure out 13 letters following a C without thinking.

As opposed to the linear memory in the event that you think you're in the roman space the only thing you need to do is glance around the room and you'll be able see when you'd like to remember! My high school bedroom to be my roman bedroom, the reason I chose this is due to the fact that this room was always cluttered and full of things. The presence of a variety of things within the room is helpful for being capable of remembering more details similar to having more landmarks can be helpful to your brain palace.

You'll want to employ the mnemonic techniques that I'll explain in the next section . They will make your mind palace as well as your roman space in the same method. There is only one difference: when you're trying to remember something , you don't have to arrange your thoughts in a specific order, instead you'll have an improvised memory system. You may find that you get more at ease with one or other system of mind palaces based on the kind of information you need to keep in mind. Make sure you cultivate both of these palaces as there could be the time when you need to recall rapidly (roman rooms) or in the order of the facts is essential in the likelihood of success(journey method)

Action item: Sit down in your Roman room (if you are able to access the actual space) and gaze at the surroundings and take in all the items. While exploring the space make sure to shut your eyes and think about scanning the space. Moving back and forth by doing this will help you to construct an accurate roman room in a short time. Once you've got an exact picture of your trip to the memory palace and your roman-themed room then move to the next step and discover how to fill your mind with palaces.

How do you fill your memory palace

In this section , we're going to explore the ways you can create a memory palace by adding objects. The idea of creating a memory castle or roman room isn't effective until you are able to collect items from the real world like objects such as numbers, quotes, or even numbers and create an abstract representation of them and store the representation in a particular area of your mind the roman room or palace. This is when most people give up on their memory palaces and quit! However, you're not the majority of people, are you? This is perhaps the most difficult part of having a memory palace. However, when you master it down, what you'll be able to recall will increase dramatically and you'll be able to use the complete method you can employ.

In this part, we'll examine how to keep in mind three distinct kinds of things. these categories will cover the majority of the items and the majority of the things you'll have to remember every day. They'll make up nearly all the things you'll use your mind for. We will cover the best ways to keep phrases and quotes and the physical items(this is the most simple) and lastly how to keep track of numbers.

One thing you'll need to be aware of when you're learning how to turn quotes and numbers into images, and transform real things and images will be that the brighter, and more emotionally charged the image you create the more likely it is to remain in your memory. If you're able to generate emotions and develop a vivid visual imagination in your mind, then the objects will be noticeable and you'll be able to remember.

How do you remember physical objects

The ability to remember physical objects is the most effective method to utilize your mind palace. This is due to the fact the fact that you have already a memory of the object. If you wish to recall it , all you need to do is pick up the object and put it within your mental palace.

One technique I employ for my mental palaces is to collect physical objects and then reduce them or increase their size so that they stand out. For instance, if you wish to keep track of your shopping list, it might be beneficial to put the various ingredients and products on your list of shopping items in your home and alter the size of them so that they help them stick out.

If you have strawberries top of your list, then you may like to imagine a huge softball-sized strawberry sitting on your chair. In changing the size this way , you could add an element of absurdity in your image, which makes it easier to recall. You don't need to stick to my advice to add emotions to your visualizations; simply remember that absurdity enhances your memory!

Another method to make things stick out is by making the color more vivid or unique. In my mind, I think of the colors as pastels. Thus, a banana that was a normal shade will soon turn shining neon yellow. When you visualize the color clearly, it not only makes the process easier for you to recall this moment it also helps strengthen the visual memory and spatial memory that will enable your mind to become more efficient in the future. If you're struggling with a specific item, I've discovered it helpful to select an absurd color. For instance, if I often miss the eggs in the supermarket I can think of a huge blue egg or an Easter egg with multiple colors to make it more absurd.

How do you remember numbers.

It is more difficult for numbers to remember than other numbers, which is due to the fact that most of us have no emotional or mental connection to numbers. The thing we'll be working to do in the next section will be understanding how to transform numbers into intriguing pictures. In this article, I'm going to present an inventory of things can help you keep track of different numbers. Also, an inventory of objects that represent different numbers. You can also use these items to add more fun and intrigue on the numbers. This list I have found useful but if you'd like to alter the items to something that is more tangible and easier to remember , you to use, then feel at ease!

One=sword since swords are lines as a 1

Two is a peace sign, because two fingers are used to create a peace symbol

Three= a teepee , because the teepee is a triangular shape and triangular triangles have three sides.

Four= a dice , because dices are squares with each side.

Five==beehive because it rhymes

Six= equals bricks since it rhymes

Seven= is heaven since it rhymes

Eight = equals an octopus since they have eight legs

Nine = equals a cat because cats live for nine years.

And zero equals hero because it rhymes

As you will see, I make associations that are simple to remember by using rhymes and other items that symbolise the numbers to me. I'd like to encourage you to make your list simple to keep in mind for yourself.

Here's how to apply this technique if you wish to recall a particular number. Let's say you want to buy some apples . your wife tells you she'd like to buy 19 apples, so I'd break the number into a number one and nine. Because one is a sword, while nine represents a cat and since we're trying to create an intense image that's why we'll imagine the cat wielding sword stabbed at an apple.

If it was in our memory palace , you could consider it to be your first place. In this way, you could think of a cat is stabbed with a sword and an apple, and in your head , you'd be able to tell that the apple was what it was and that your wife is asking to purchase 19 of the. (why she's so specific can't be explained to me!)

It is a great method to keep track of numbers. Remember that when you write the list, which are different from mine, you should make the same pictures every time to make it easier and you will also need to pick interesting things since they make it easier to remember scenes.

Before proceeding to the practice section let's look at a second instance. If you were trying to remember the full number, such as 10,941, you can break it down in this way. 1 sword, 0 hero, 9 cat, 4 dice, 1 sword again. It is possible to imagine a sword hung on a wall. Then a Greek hero appears and grabs the sword. He walks up to a cat shooting dice and cuts dice in half using his sword. Through creating a short film within your mind by doing this, you will be able to recall the numbers in order. If you're able to recall them, all you need to do is remember the story, then identify it (which will become faster and faster as you make use of your list.

If you're eager to give this technique a go right now, read the following list, and if you're feeling confident, attempt to recall the number and name of each object. If you're just beginning with your mind-based palace, you may find it simpler and more efficient to keep track of the things you'll need by putting the items on your way to the walls of your palace.

Here's your list of exercises Place it in your castle Best of luck!

36 eggs

Five Apple's

2 tubes of toothpaste

Toilet paper

1 1-pound chicken breasts

Three asparagus bundles

Chili powder

2 bottles olive oils

Dog treats

18 coca Cola's

Aspirin in one bottle

Three bars of candy.

How do I remember quotes?

When you're trying to imagine quotes, you'll go through the same thing as you're making up numbers. The main thing to remember is to create a picture that you can use to recall the quote. In my mind, I frequently make a persona of the person who is saying the phrase. Here's an illustration.

One of my favourite works" the illusions" written by Richard Bach one of the characters talks about the realities of. The protagonist is a pilot who flies with a biplane throughout the country and gives people rides while showing them areas from up above. In the story , he is the messiah, and has the capability to swim on the water as well as other feats like that. This quote is a simple one that says this

"It's all a lie, Richard"

It's an easy quote, however one of the ways I was able to connect the quote with the book was to imagine in my head that the character flying down from above , and an aircraft landing in a field , jumping out of the plane , wearing an illusionist outfit and gesturing lavishly to everyone surrounding him, while uttering the phrase.

It's evident it's a great method to generate more emotion about the quotation. Let's look at another quote to understand the way you'll create emotions and images about your own quotations. Roman philosophers Seneca was said to have said

"Set aside a set amount of days during which you'll be satisfied with the tiniest and least expensive menu, wearing a course and rough clothing, saying to yourself"Is this the situation I was dreading?"

As I think of this quote , I am thinking of four elements: the time-saving to days off, most slender and least expensive of meals and the most rough dress and finally is this the one that I was dreading?

Let's break it down so that you can be aware that you need to make a set amount of days in each month. I picture Seneca at a table in his palace, with his calendar and a sharpie red marker, making X marks on days when you will be practicing his worst-case scenario.

To help me keep track of the next section I'm imagining that he visits the market and pays only a penny gets the bread wheel. This is the most affordable part of the quotation.

The fun begins where I picture him in "course and rough clothing" I imagine him wearing an outfit made of sandpaper sheets, which have been joined.

Finally, to think of the fear aspect, I can imagine Seneca laughing in a mocking way at the gown made of sandpaper and then shaking his fist towards the sky and shouting "Is this the situation I was afraid of?"

I hope that from these two examples you'll be able to consider ways you can turn your own quotes into images or stories. The thing I've noticed is that rather than attempt to keep the different elements of the quote as distinct items within your memory palace, I think of a film that plays in my mind and the location of the film is usually within my mind palace.

A few fun quotes to remember

You should set aside a specific amount of days during which you will be satisfied with the tiniest and least expensive menu, wearing a course and rough clothing while you ask yourself all as you go: "Is this the condition that I was expecting?"

"You appear to be mortal in all you are afraid of and as immortals in everything you wish to be"

Seneca

"People are very careful when it comes to guarding their personal belongings, however, when they begin to waste their time they're most squanderful of the only area that is proper to be greedy."

Seneca

Friendship isn't necessary, as is the philosophy of art, or even the art... It's not worth the risk of survival but it is one of the things that are essential to the idea of survival.

C.S. Lewis

The philosophy of a person isn't best expressed through words; it's expressed through the choices we make... And the choices we make are our own responsibility.

Eleanor Roosevelt

Chapter 3: The Brain Food

Omega 3 fat acids

Recent studies of college students have shown that eating Omega 3 fatty acids in fish oil pills each for a few months enhanced their working memory by 20%. This is an amazing boost to memory from a single compound and a great sign for us who are aspiring Sherlock Holmes'. Omega 3 fats can help decrease inflammation in the brain and speed up the flow of blood throughout the body (and which also includes brain)

Some of the sources are fish oil, fish the nuts, nut butters avocados, and many other. Consuming all of these food items every day can help you get healthier and boost brain function . But lets face it, a diet consisting of avocados and salmon can be expensive quickly. If you'd like to enjoy to reap all the benefits at only a fraction of the cost you can supplement with 2000mg of fish oil daily as did the participants in the study. In addition to eating this high intake of omega-3 fats, you will be less prone to the chance of developing degenerative mental illnesses such as Alzheimer's

Plenty of water

Studies of college students who took tests have shown the students drinking plenty of water and hydrated during the tests they took the test scored 10% more than students who weren't.

Drinking water can do more than quell thirst. Water is your body's most effective method to eliminate contaminants in the body. Also, drinking more water will rid your body of toxic substances that impact the way your brain performs. Furthermore water is the principal method by which oxygen gets to the brain, which is why drinking plenty of water is vital for optimal brain function.

Dark greens and Berries

Dark greens such as kale, collard greens, as well as spinach contain high amounts of vitamin E and folate. Although it's unclear exactly what these two substances do to protect the brain , research indicates that inflammation and death of cells in the brain are less when we eat a diet that is full of vitamins E as well as folate.

Berries can be beneficial in helping to ensure that the body is functioning properly in the process of removing toxins from our blood. There is no way to know how this happens however, when people consume more fruit, the damage associated with toxins are greatly diminished.

Supplements to improve memory

Coffee

I know what you're thinking. Duh. It is true that coffee is an enhancing drink for performance. Naturally, I'm planning to drink it to improve my memory just like college students have since the beginning of time. Here's the information you may not be aware of the reason coffee is effective and how you can use it properly.

Are you still here? There's a wrong method to drink coffee? Yes. And I, you as well as the majority of the world are guilty of it!

The caffeine in coffee is stimulant. this is a big portion of what gives you all that energy boost, but what many people don't realize is that it also creates blood vessels in your body larger, thereby pumping more blood throughout the organs (and the brain.) It's important to note that coffee has this impact if you drink approximately 12oz of the beverage!

Many of us believe that more is better. If one cup makes me feel more clear than three cups, then it must be more beneficial. However, coffee can make the blood vessels inside our bodies smaller after drinking several cups. If you'd like to feel energized and never tired, but stop the circulation of blood to the brain, take a break and drink a few cups of coffee. However, for those who are like me and wish to to remember things as long as you can and to have a healthy brain, limit your coffee consumption to around one cup every six hours.

Nicotine gum (for the experimenter)

If you're a hardcore biohacker who is seeking greater risks to improve performance, then nicotine may be a good option for you. *Note I don't endorse any particular activity, I simply would like to share my thoughts. Nicotine is widely known as a stimulant, and also for cause cancer, right? The cancer-causing substances in the majority of nicotine-based products (think chewing gum and smoking cigarettes) aren't the nicotine, but rather the burning matter of plants, tar and other ingredients.

Nicotine by itself is far less harmful to your body than the other components in most mixes. As an aside, Nicotine might just be one of the most effective intelligent drugs available.

One of the effects: Nicotine increases your IQ

In this study , researchers examined two different groups of people through the IQ test. The smokers' results showed significantly higher IQ which led to conclude that nicotine increased the capacity of people to process information fast.

Second effect The speed of reaction is increased.

Another intriguing benefit of inhaling nicotine, either in gum or patches is that your response time is actually monitored. If you're a person who plays sports or driving in tough conditions, this could be an extremely useful method. The ability to reduce your reaction time is important in many sports as well as tea, and can help you stay safe when driving. I've had a personal experience of this. For about a month, I chewed nicotine gum on a daily basis in order to enjoy the claimed advantages. I was driving late at evening and a deer leapt over my head. I was able to dodge the deer, even though my choice of action might not be the right one, as applying brakes could have been the safer option. However, I was astonished by my own reaction time and it felt like I was reacting immediately.

Third effect third effect: nicotine can enhance your handwriting.

It's a fascinating result of using nicotine however, the research that accompanied it found that smoking nicotine may help you write faster and more precisely. This is in line with my own experiences when I took nicotine. the main thing I wanted to try was note-taking and reading abilities, but that after taking the nicotine gum at 4 mg tablet, within a half hour I was buzzing , and writing a quicker. In addition, my handwriting was more neat! My handwriting is that of doctors. Most people aren't able to read it, but when I was smoking nicotine, my handwriting was pretty clear.

In general, I'd say is you're seeking to improve your performance, particularly your ability to reduce you reaction speed and speed up the processing of information like writing or reading and writing, then nicotine gum is a good choice as a short-term solution. Of course , you're not going be able to use often and end up becoming addicted however, I've found that a small chewing gum that contains nicotine does much more than all the cups coffee will ever achieve. It is my intention to keep using it as a study aid in the near future.

Piracetam+ Choline

The last item on our checklist of vitamins that can help boost your brain's performance are two classics from the past such as piracetam and Choline. These two supplements are always combined due to their effects on your body. The first supplement piracetam is believed to improve your capacity to learn. Additionally, it creates more vivid and vivid sensations, your hearing gets sharper and your vision becomes clearer.

Piracetam Works by stimulating the neurons in your brain , increasing the probability that they'll start firing. In addition, it increases the frequency of firing that the brain's nerves Piracetam can ensure that you can be more efficient and clear in your thinking The only drawback to this is that when you're taking piracetam, your brain is actually using excessive energy!

If you don't take it with having any choline at all, it's like trying to drive in a tiniest amount of gas in the fastest way you can! Due to this, many people (myself including myself) take choline supplements. Choline is the main substance in the body. It is later converted into the neurotransmitter acetylcholine , which is the most important neurotransmitter by the brain. When you combine both supplements you'll be able to think more clearly and more quickly. The primary aspect I noticed was that by that by taking both supplements, I was able to increase my ability to process words.

I did a reading speed test prior to taking choline and piracetam and I was reading around 150 words per minute which is slightly quicker than the typical college student. After taking these supplements for approximately an entire week, I went to the same test and read around 1100 words/minute, with no loss of comprehension. It's an impressive result but I am of the opinion that one of the reasons I could read faster was due to the belief that I could read more quickly. But, piracetam and choline are both known to have an extremely powerful impact on how the brain works. Being one of the oldest known drugs available and a drug that is used to treat Alzheimer's disease, piracetam is an excellent option for those who want to learn more and perform better each day. I highly recommend the use of piracetam.

Chapter 4: It Also Helps To Strengthen Memory

The brain and cardio

Exercise is among the most crucial aspects of your life that you have be aware of if you wish to improve your brain's performance. Studies have proven that for those who do one hour of cardio each week, three times per week for six months , there is an impressive increase in their brains and the density. Through cardio, they strengthen the brain as an muscle.

The reason why aerobic exercise can boost your brain and creates the drastic effects is because when you perform cardio , there are a number of things that happen that boost brain growth. The obvious and primary reason is that when you exercise, you're pumping blood more throughout your body. This circulation of blood increases the quantity of nutrients and oxygen delivered to every part of your body. When your brain is receiving greater amounts of oxygen and nutrients. will likely to increase as a response to stimuli (learning)

The other reason for the cardio to be effective in improving brain function is that exercise triggers production of serotonin as well as dopamine. These chemicals can make you feel happy and lessen stress. Through stimulating the release of these two hormones, we are better able to concentrate because the stress you've experienced in your life has been eliminated by your workout.

The last reason exercise is efficient in helping you concentrate and increase your abilities to learn is when you jog, run, and sprint, your body triggers the release of norepinephrine, a hormone that is called adrenaline. What people don't realize is that drinking a cup of coffee can have similar effects! Caffeine can stimulate the body's adrenaline levels, but through cardio, you can achieve the same effect you're in a position to feel an uplifting sensation. This is why , after running for long distances, many people do not feel tired, they feel high!

Research has proven that if you take the time to study immediately following exercise, you will be able to keep 20 percent more information. A further 20% may not sound like much however, when you add all the tiny 20% improvement throughout the entire book , they add up to a significant improvement within your brain. Don't be shocked if you find yourself able to recall many times more information once you have practiced all the techniques included in this guide.

A short-term boost in nitro and efficient cardio

One of the most remarkable advantages of doing cardio not only its long-lasting health advantages however, the fact that when you begin learning right when you do cardio, you'll learn more quickly and at a higher speed. The ability to problem solve and the ability to comprehend increase by around 20% following exercises that involve cardio. However, what's fascinating is that not every exercise counts. Low-intensity cardio, like running, gentle swimming or even riding a bicycle isn't as effective in the mind as high intensity cardiovascular.

Be assured that I'm not going to leave you in the dark. I'll give you a few guidelines that are helpful for getting an amazing cardio workout that will help your brain and heart efficiently in a very short amount of time.

The technique I'm going to show you is referred to as the high-intensity interval training, or high intensity interval training for short. This kind of training is focused on providing a full-on intensive effort over a short amount of time, followed by an interval of rest. If you follow this method and exercise with intervals such as this, you can get an intense cardio workout within a short period of time. It does not matter which type of cardio workout you pick. You can pick from swimming, running cycling, or jumping, the most important thing is adhering to these fundamentals

The first principle is to do everything you can When you're doing the exercise, make sure you give it 95-100 percent of your energy. If you exercise this, you will be able to feel short of breath after just 20 or 30 seconds.

Principle two, exercise twice while you rest When you're doing this kind of cardio, a best practice is to work for 20 seconds, and then take a break for around 10 seconds.

Third principle: use an alarm clock, be real: what's important in this type of exercise that you utilize an alarm clock because it's easy to let yourself cheat out of a small amount of time that passes by. This is the timer I use to do my workouts. Action item Once you've mastered the basics of how to perform HIIT, it's time to implement this method and begin the first high intensity Interval training session. To do this, you need to choose an exercise you are able to do with some intensity (I love jumping rope) and then do one timer that I've demonstrated to you using these three principles in your mind. If you follow this method, you'll be able to get a effective workout in just 4 minutes!

Chapter 5: The Reasons We Struggle To Recall

"I will only say how beautiful the past was since there is no way to feel that they are feeling emotions at the moment. It grows later so we don't feel completely regarding the present, but only in the past."

-- Virginia Woolf

L

Let's talk about all the issues associated with memory and the reasons we often forget. We'll concentrate on common causes that cause difficulties remembering things.

Apart from the simple aging process There are many factors that cause memory loss. We will address the real difficulties that people experience in retaining their memories. For the elderly, we usually blame memory problems on decline of the body and the aging process, such as dementia and Alzheimer's disease.

However, even though many people are in their 20s and enjoy good mental health there are times when we forget things. Here are a few reasons for that:

Poor Retrieval

Sometimes, you can't recall an experience or a description of something.

The feeling that you are sure you've remembered something, but the memory has disappeared. The reason for this is the brain's inability to retrieve stored memories. This could be due to an inability to focus when remembering or as a sign of something much more serious. It is usually due to a glitch in the encoding process and is easily fixed by a few easy techniques.

The Decay Theory

Forgetfulness is one of the main reasons that people are having difficulty remembering. The term decay theory can be used to describe the idea of slow recovery. The theory behind decay says that a part or memory "decays" when an individual creates a new memory. It is widely acknowledged that neurons die gradually as we age, however, some of the older memories could be more robust than more recent ones. The theory of decay is primarily based on our short-term memory systems which suggests that old memories are more resilient to shocks or retained in the event of physical assaults to the brain. While the memory may be somewhere, we tend to bury it under the recent memories we've added. In time, that memory will vanish when there is no effort to recall. In simple terms the decay theory states that you forget things that don't practice or repeat. This memory "decays" and is then erased.

The Encouraged Forgetfulness Program or Suppression

People offer inspirational quotations and inspirational speeches to suffering or depressed person. However, the person who is suffering might want to forget about the painful memories. I refer to this as "encouraged memory." This idea suggests that we help a person to forget about their most difficult experiences. This is an occurrence that happens naturally in a society that regularly is struggling to cope with painful and past sorrow. Any memory that contributes to your "worst times" in your life isn't the most encouraging one. A lot of people are prone to throw the memories away' so that they don't dwell on the past.

After a break-up, the loss of a loved ones or ill-luck, or a failure during a test that is crucial to your school All you want be able to focus on forgetting. You'd rather not think about them to be at peace. The urge to'move forward and forget that it ever occurred' is just one of the reasons people forget. It is also possible to forget the memory prior to or following the trauma. We do our best to forget these thoughts, so that we don't drown in anxiety. It is exhausting and rude and can cause a lot of harm to the mind and the heart. Naturally we seek to avoid discomfort and get rid of it.

According to some PSYCHOLOGISTS
According to some psychologists, conscious forgetting of the painful memory is considered to be suppression. Unconsciously forgetting an unpleasant memory is an act of repression. There are a few psychologists who believe in the theory of repression due to the difficulties in studying memory that is repressed.

Interference

The same way interference could block the radio's signal In psychology, the interference can cause confusion in memories. It's not a deliberate effort to erase a memory, but the result of mixing several memories. Two events that are similar could be mixed up when your brain focuses on the most beautiful or the most recent. This is a way of filtering your thoughts and creating memories, which can bring out the false memory.

Information Overload

This is the result of learning the information first, and then getting additional information. If this happens, it makes it more difficult for our brain to remember the information we have learned since it was unable to take in the new information before we added additional information over it. The best option is to break up the new bits of information. Like a break between sets in the fitness center, our minds require some time to recharge before studying more material.

The memory of old times is forgotten

We often forget an old memory simply because we are surrounded by new memories. The need to concentrate on "the present" somehow occurs to us in a way that is not conscious. We're in the present and trying to adjust to a new environment and this can lead to the forgetting of old memories.

Making new memories and forgetting them

A CHANGE IN PERSONALITY CAN OCCUR
An old memory might be one that you'll be able to remember instead of a new one. It's because memories could be more significant and meaningful to you.

The NBC television series "This is Us" portrays Rebecca Pearson as someone who is unable to remember simple things such as where she put her phone. However, she is able to remember every minute of her first motherhood days. The time was more precious to her than current times, and that could be the case to us as well. It is possible to cherish the memories of earlier times because they were great moments.

LIKEWISE Majid Fotuhi writes of a brain tumor that was discovered in 1940 operation that was performed in the Montreal Neurological Institute in Canada. Brenda Milner, PhD. is a Psychology professor, collaborated together with Wilder Penfield, M.D. an neurosurgeon, during the procedure. In the course of their work, Dr. Milner observed that these patients were having difficulty recalling or recording new memories. However, they were able to recall the most important memories of their lives.

The patients who came to see and had a conversation with her, would not remember her once she went away and returned just a few minutes later. Patients would frequently beg to differ with the joke, even after having it repeated three or four times. They would laugh as if they'd never heard of it before. It's also a matter of being able to acquire fresh data (Fotuhi). This is due to the operation to remove the hippocampus. It is an organ of the brain that assists in memory. If a person's hippocampus fails to perform its purpose, they might forget newer memories. However, they'll be able retain older memories.

Insufficiency of Interest

Certain memories are more important in comparison to others. so we typically put a label on the memory. If someone is interested in a certain object, they will try to keep it in mind. If a particular moment isn't of any interest it's not a priority to keep the memory. The interest is based on a specific event or person that is significant in our lives. It's not the fault of you if you're not interested. But it causes people to forget about the least interesting individuals or even events.

Time passing (Transience)

When time passes by memories are lost and that's the reason we forget. It is inevitable that we forget one or the other as a lot of things are a constant distraction. In Psychology the term "transience" is used to describe this period in time to be "transience."

The process of passing time causes many changes. One of it is the capacity to recall specific memories. A typical adult human is able to store around 2.5 millions of gigabytes. What's odd is that memory sometimes disappears the following day or even a week later. After an entire year, is it acceptable that you'll forget an event, but do you remember an item on the following day? Brain scientists have argued that this issue of memory is beneficial. The reason is that the brain filters the flood of memories and focuses on the most important ones. I don't agree with this with this. I prefer to keep a record of every detail.

Too often, I think.

A PERSON who is a thinker to the max on the world's issues may have trouble with memory loss as well. Analyzing and thinking is good however it can affect your memory significantly when you think too much about certain subjects.

A person with depression may be suffering from memory problems. Being depressed and forgetting things can be detrimental to the brain. If you're depressed and want to talk to a therapist you can locate one who specializes in the field of memory recovery.

False attribution (Failure in Recalling the Complete Details)

Now, there are situations in which a person has to lose the data intended to be stored. It's not usually deliberate but rather, it's due to an inability to store information within the brain. The memory hasn't had the chance to be stored in your head and, as a result you've lost the ability to recall it. Sometimes, we don't realize that the memory has disappeared from our mind. Small details such as the car's color could disappear from our minds. The only thing we can remember is the dimensions of the automobile. The chair of Harvard University's Psychology Department, Daniel Schacter published a book entitled The Seven Sins of Memory The Mind's Way of Forgetting and Recalls. Schacter also mentions misattribution as a kind of memory loss.

Sleep levels

Based on a study conducted by the HARVARD-BASED NURSES' study written by Howard Lewine, "too little sleep, as well as excessive amounts of sleep can affect brain's memory." This study found that those who don't get enough sleeping at night are often suffering from problems with blood flow, which reduces the brain's capacity to retain memories. In the same way, those who are getting an excessive amount of sleep tend to forget too.

Insufficient sleep can affect your ability to remember information. Your brain is fatigued and weak, so it requires some time to rest. It's simple to comprehend the effects of poor sleep on memory. However, it can be difficult to grasp how many nights of sleep can impact your memory. The people who suffer from this suffer from "poor health sleep" (Harvard Health). It is important to consider the best ways to control your sleep so that you can increase your performance and memory.

Inattention to detail

Remembering is an act of recording, storing, and recollecting information. Inattention can cause people to forget. If we do not pay attention to something, an event or even people then the brain won't be able to store the information in its memory areas correctly. In the end, if you're required to recall an event that is not significant that happened in your lifetime, you'll likely forget the event. For instance, you might remember the you had for dinner in the past or the day before. If the food wasn't memorable, you'll likely forget about it.

There is a reason why we aren't able to recall that is more significant than all other. This is the reason that can cause the desperation of the most powerful women and men. It could cause them to fail to achieve their goals, goals, or goals. In the next part we will look at the power of belief and the reasons it is the most crucial factor to gain control over your memory.

The ability to harness your belief system is the basis for everything amazing you'd like to accomplish in your life. If you're looking to have the ability to remember the powers of a or chess player, then you need to take the first step is controlling your thoughts and your mind. Being mindful provides you with the ultimate advantage over the way your memory functions and how much focus you focus on the important things that are important in your life.

Let me demonstrate how to manage your thoughts and your mind in just three easy steps:

Do Mindful Meditation

Not everyone believes that this method works in any way. A few people I've spoken to have made excuses for being incapable of concentrating. If you're one of them, or even thought of using that as a reason to excuse yourself it's the first thing that you must to remove from your mind as it's not true. Meditation works. It is a method by which you can learn to center your attention on things that are not part of the physical world.

According to a study conducted in a study conducted by Harvard researchers According to a study by Harvard researchers, Meditation can reduce stress, insomnia, boost productivity, lessen distractions and anxiety, improve wellbeing and stress, and increase the quality of life. If you're interested in learning how to control and master your thoughts, emotions, and mind, you need to take the time to practice meditation.

Be aware of your thoughts.

DO NOT GUESS; simply take note of. There are times when your head should be considered with a full focus. Some thoughts should be flushed out. Have you ever worked involved in a project in the office and during that time , you recall the time you swam in the ocean prior as well as how waves made your board navigate the ocean? These thoughts have no place in a space like the workplace, particularly when dealing with a significant task. What you must do is to observe and let the thought go. It's in the process of thinking about the idea and then reminiscing on what happened that you can get lost. It is important to be focused when you think.

Create a Space for Aligning Your Mind and Thoughts

By saying this I was implying that you should give be able to give your mind a clear direction to be in sync the thoughts of your mind. This way, you're growing with what Gerald Edelman called "the primary consciousness," which underlies all thoughts.

CLAUDE DEBUSSY's analogy is clear meaning in all its ramifications. According to the French composer, it's the "space between notes that make the music understandable." This means there is no space in which the sound would not be able to make sense in the first place. When you are in this state of consciousness the mind is cleared of any thoughts that are distracting you and reach a state of calm and complete concentration. So, until you reach the level of consciousness you desire it's very difficult to manage your thoughts.

Chapter 6: The Power Of Beliefs

"Strength is the result of a formulated mind." John Beecher. John Beecher

A

The subtitle of the chapter suggests the title of this chapter says, we're about to discover how to harness our minds in order to develop our memory. It is equally possible to have discussed the power of beliefs into the previous chapter, since there's nothing more damaging to our development than self-limiting beliefs. But, just as the mind's influence can negatively to impact our performance, it can also do the reverse is the case. The mind is an extremely powerful part of our bodies and can help us achieve amazing accomplishments if we can only learn to make use of it. Before we get into the power of our mind we need to discuss the negative self-beliefs that keep us back, and the source they originate.

Every day every day we are bombarded by advertisements and other media that claim we're insufficient or less than we are because we don't have this or excessive amounts of this or that. It's not fair to be angry at the businesses or advertisers for doing what they must for the purpose of selling an item. In addition the negative perception of marketing is only the surface in our assumptions. Marketing is often based on hope, however, marketing experts have learned that the fear of loss is the main motivational factor. There are a variety of flaws in our hard-working exterior that allow negative thoughts to get in.

Self-defeating thoughts can halt our progress before it begins. It is possible that we grew up in a home that saw family members tear us down and said that we would never be able to achieve our goals. Maybe the problem is "friends" who rather than help your confidence, pulled you down. You may still have those "friends." The internal anxiety and self-defeating attitude can come from a variety of sources. However, instead of focusing on the problems instead, let's look at the solution.

LET'S create our minds into an ever-growing castle which continue to build our faith in ourselves. Let's develop the strong mental attitude needed to build the highest level of memory.

We all know people who view their world in a perpetual battle with odds that are constantly stacking up against them. Take a look at that person now. Are things going the way they want or does their thinking turn into self-fulfilling prophecies? When I consider the stereotyped negative Nancy (Sorry to anyone who are reading the article) in my life, they don't appear to be able to make things happen as planned. They are always failing before they even begin and, frequently rather than taking the blame for their own actions they blame the problem to things that are never within their control.

As well, I know people who, despite huge obstacles overcome and appear to transform challenges into opportunities. The primary difference between these kinds of people is usually simply their attitude and what they believe. To have the mindset required to attain amazing results in our memory, it is necessary to begin with the correct mental attitude. Let's start with a crucial question to establish the scene.

So now that you understand the reasons you'd like to improve your memory, let's look at common myths that surround our memory.

Myth 1

I was not born with a sharp memory, and I'll always be in a state of forgetfulness.

It's a lie! We are blessed with extraordinary memories. This is why babies are able to absorb information like sponges. From the moment they're born to around 3 years of age, kids possess the capacity to absorb new things and keep them in their memory. But that does not mean that if you've grown up, you're out of luck. This means that you need to be more diligent and allow yourself more opportunities to keep important information in front of you. Every person was born with the capacity to retain specifics and details and can all improve their memory capacity. possess. You may not make it into the Guinness Book of World Records for being able to recall the numbers of pi. However, you could be able to recall the names of every person you meet.

Myth 2

My brain can only store the information it needs; if I have learned one thing and forget the next.

Our brains can hold more information than even the most powerful supercomputers. This means that you can pack a lifetime's worth of information and knowledge inside your brain, and be able to add more. When you have mastered the right method of encoding, storage and retrieval that is right for you, you can use the knowledge that you probably would have forgotten decades ago.

Myth 3

Certain lucky people have photography memories, but I am not one of them.

The majority of scientists agree that photographic memory doesn't exist. It's a popular phrase invented by someone else however, it's not really true. Certain people naturally have more memory than other people. That's the beauty of living; it isn't a factor in the world how other people do. It's all that matters is that you grow your performance from the point you were yesterday. In the present the only person you're fighting with is staring at you from the mirror. Memory champions aren't gifted with a superpower. They are naturally gifted minds that have been sharpened over hundreds of hours of study and Mnemonic devices. There have been numerous studies that have proven that the individuals who have the best memory were not able to achieve their achievements only because of luck. They were hard at work for years studying their craft, and discovering every trick to master their minds. You can learn and practice all they learned!

Myth 4

Memories are a thing that is fixed and cannot alter.

We can alter memories without even making an effort. You can recall things the same way, but after a long period of time and external influences, we are able to alter the way we remember things in our brains. Feelings and emotions, as well as beliefs you hold influence the past memories that are stored in your brain. It is our responsibility to be aware of both internal and external forces which could alter memory and render it less trustworthy. We'll be taught how to avoid misremembering later on in this book.

Myth 5

Your memory functions as a camera that records events to replay in the future.

This is a simplified view of the reality. Because we are living creatures that experience emotions, dramas as well as physical and emotional changes like we've said earlier that our memories may undergo subtle changes. It's normal, and it is crucial to develop the ability to store information in a manner which stops this from occurring. Without a systematic approach to your memory it's quite likely that your mind's recording doesn't match what the camera could have seen through its lens.

Myth 6

If I'm not able to learn through visuals, I will never be a strong memory.

It's not what we see through our eyes that is important. It's what we perceive through our minds, and how we perceive the information that we're bombarded by. The information that we tend to remember the most is that which we perceive using more than just our eyes. The more sensory inputs you can engage in coding memories, the more efficient. Consider the senses we use as triggers. You may remember a slice of cheesecake if it was visible all around you. If you smelt the fresh scent of cheesecake, grabbed a handful by the hand and slid the delicious cold cheesecake into your mouth, you'd have stimulated more of your senses and thus enhanced the memory of the time. While it isn't possible to always use all five senses when encoding, you can try to make sure you engage all five senses as you can. Through practice, you may even attempt to fool your brain into engaging sensitivities you weren't able to use to!

Now that we have debunked a variety of myths that ignorant public believes regarding memory, I'll highlight a few points you must know and absorb.

* You were born with an incredible memory, and the ability to store your information in your brain is there.

* Science says that memory is the key to a healthy life, therefore a better memory can make you happier.

Once you commit towards improving memory you'll be able to see improvement in areas you'd never imagined.

* You'll never fill your brain to capacity So you will be able to learn each and each day. Your mind is capable of accommodating any amount or level of information that you provide it.

* If you are about to be exposed to something completely complex and new then you should prepare your brain to be prepared. Like a vaccine that helps us prepare for a greater dose of a virus an exposure of a tiny amount to something new helps for us for more knowledge about it later on.

Failure is simply feedback. If you've forgotten something you promised to keep in mind, don't be discouraged. Examine the reasons for what happened and then figure out how to avoid the same scenario for the next time. This way, you can enhance your thinking with each positive and negative outcome. This is what separates the great from the average.

I hope you can realize the wonderful possibility that is waiting for you. If you're eager to change your life and build not only your memory, but the entire brain now is the time to make it happen.

The reason you're looking to boost your memory and what it can do throughout your life.

Why Would You Like to Enhance Your Memory

"A good photograph keeps an instant from disappearing."

-- E. Welty

W

If improving your memory can bring a variety of advantages, it's something that's easy to attain. Humans are naturally inclined to forget. To address this issue it is first necessary to recognize what it is that we'd like to achieve in order to build an amazing memory. Find out the reason behind making a change. It is important to understand the implications of having a more efficient memory can mean for our lives.

A BETTER STORY means we'll be more in control of our lives. It will transform how we view the world. It will help develop the brain's ability to focus, our concentration and the ability to make smart choices. Additionally, a better memory will allow you to make the right decision fast. We can be able to better adapt to the changing conditions and solve issues and difficulties easily.

Whatever field of the world we live in, having a stronger memory can be beneficial. A better memory can transform our social, personal emotional, academic or professional lifestyles.

Personal Life

A better memory can aid you in becoming a better an individual. It is possible to combine all the important memories of your life and help remain calm in the face of crisis.

Sometimes, you need to grow in your work as well as your attitude and your mental outlook. If you have a good memory, these aspects will come together. A good memory aids in plan your life's goals and also helps you gain knowledge from the past. It also assists us in weaving a beautiful tapestry of our past filled with memories that we want to never forget, as well as moments that bring us joy. Memories are a bridge between the present and the past and allow us to observe growth, progress and transformation in a linear manner.

Aids in the Management of Plans

If an amazing idea pops up and you remember it, you'll be able to create plans to implement the idea. A strong memory can help to remember the areas of your life you are able to alter and the steps to take.

In the next chapter in this book, you'll be taught how to build your memory. In this means you'll know how to make plans in a way that is efficient.

Learning Lessons From History

The mistakes we've made in our past help us navigate the present. The saying goesthat "we are taught from the mistakes we make." However, If you can't recall your mistakes, will you be able to learn from them?

Memories of MISTAKES can be a source of pain for US But they also assist us in moving forward, while avoiding repeating the same mistakes. Sometimes, we must be aware of our past mistakes in order to stay in place and avoid getting distracted over and over again by mistakes.

With BETTER control on your memories, you will be able to save important memory from your past. Sometimes bad and other times good recalling the past can in determining our future. It's especially true If you're able to manage negative memories and apply them to enrich your present and your future lives.

Increases Creativity

A better memory can boost your creative abilities and it helps you make the right choices. A lot of times, people who are creative use ideas they've seen and elsewhere. Therefore, recollecting these ideas will spark your imagination. There are many innovative ideas from others which can be used to aid us in overcoming challenges and create opportunities. This makes you come up with innovative ways to create something fresh.

Social Life

HAVING BETTER memories can help you improve your social life. In social gatherings, gatherings and gatherings the sharp memory of yours can be a big help in avoiding awkward situations, such as not remembering the face of someone after speaking to them, or not being able to remember names of people. Social interactions is more effective, because you'll be able to remember the majority of the conversations you engage in with others.

When you remember your friends You can expand your circle of social acquaintances. This is because, as in social interactions the conversation flow. Inability to identify the face of a person is known as prosopagnosia. You're not able to recognize the structure of the face of the person in order to identify their face in the future. This could cause awkwardness when the person is seen in another location.

Being Better at Love

Being able to remember more can help you live a more satisfying love life. The ability to remember important information that can enhance your love life is essential. A lot of breakups are caused by the inability to remember and it's a very reality. The most damaging part is that a forgotten experience frequently becomes a memory your partner will never forget. Making amends to past mistakes is one method by which a more positive memory could affect your life's emotional state. Perhaps it's simply as simple as remembering that you had dinner plans, and turning up at the right time. Whatever the case, a great memory can make a huge impact on someone special.

Academic Life

We all know that schools were created to facilitate the instruction of formal subjects that you may never use. But what happens if we find out that what we learn can help us in the future, if we just keep them in mind? Learning and remembering lessons is an essential part of each school's goals. Learn about the lessons, the duties and everything else that impact your grades at the school. A great memory will help you remember the lessons learned and will improve upon it in preparation for a real test. The best part is that it could be useful in your future!

Being More Intelligent

When you've got a greater memory than an academic, you are able to connect various concepts and theories. There is no limit to any one subject since you're aware of the many aspects of the subject. It's not just about getting excellent grades. You also have an enlightened mind that can capture a variety of thoughts.

In class, you may even be more interested if you're separated into groups. Also, you can ask your professor smart questions when you need to. A lot of the time, students who study for exams don't receive the top scores. But those who really know a subject are the ones who score A's. It's because they're not working on the short-term memory, in which they must remember the information. They are able to transfer the knowledge they've learned to their long-term and medium-term memory. This has the added benefit of actually learning something for the future too.

Being more reliable

The benefits of having a better memory don't limit you to getting high marks or becoming the smartest person in class. If you're serious about your academics, your professors would recommend you to anybody. They'll also have faith in you for any task. That's because you've got an extremely sharp memory.

There is nothing more satisfying than having a group of friends who are adamant about you, especially if these individuals could assist you in the future because you demonstrated an ability to comprehend the subject while others struggled to remember it.

Better Stage Present

There are some classes in the school curriculum that require an audience as well, and when you've developed an impressive memory, it will be simple for you to remember. Many claim to suffer from fear of speaking in a or stage performance. This is due to "being scared of not remembering." While others may be afraid of the sheer amount of people in the audience they are surrounded by, you might be worried about not remembering your lines. This happens frequently. Once you've developed your memory and are able to recall every aspect to be considered when you're delivering your speech. Your confidence is crucial however, a great memory can boost your confidence!

Learn New Concepts in class

A better memory will allow you to have the ability to master new concepts at the classroom. Paula Fiet, a student researcher at Weber State University, discovered that short-term memory is the reason many students struggle to grasp new concepts in the classroom. A lot of students aren't able to grasp the concepts that are taught in Maths, Physics, Literature and Geography. They aren't able to retain the facts, even if teachers have explained the concept many times.

She ADDS that you need to have a working memory to grasp these difficult concepts. She further states "Children who don't have a good working memory don't have enough information stored in their heads to understand what's entering their minds." This means that students who are classified as slow learners in the classroom have difficulties in their memory. This is why many parents opt for the idea of homeschooling or private tutoring for their children. It is essential to be constantly informed about their lessons But what happens is the best option if their memory isn't strong enough? It is best to improve your memory to be able to learn new concepts.

Professional Life

Believe it or not Remembering can also enhance you in your work. Imagine what a stronger memory can do for the workplace or with your customers. Recalling important facts, figures and obstacles can help your boss remember when a promotion is due.

Better Focus

Sometimes at WORK you'll find yourself with a lot of tasks to complete and all you need to do is concentrate. The ability to connect details is essential for a successful work environment. Every day, we are pulled into a myriad of directions; it's easy to lose track of important goals and deadlines. Better memory will enable you to focus better on the tasks you have to complete at work. You won't get lost in the tasks you need to complete.

With a better focus With a better focus, you can learn how to use equipment that you've never used before. Sometimes, we discover new skills during our work. It's our responsibility to figure out the solution and remembering our experiences can aid. For example there are tables used within the Word document. It is necessary to insert an Excel spreadsheet in it. It is likely that there will be a way to insert an Excel spreadsheet. Perhaps you're only aware of that you were taught the concept in a computer class at middle school. Imagine how much time you could save in the event that you could recall the information.

A BETTER MEMORY can help you be more creative. It also brings creative ideas to the workplace. It will impress your employees by your dedication to making the company more advanced. It proves you're reliable and that's what companies are looking for in a potential CEO.

Lower Dependence on Machines that Sometimes fail

We all know that technology is more likely to fail in times of require it. In this connected world there will come a time that you just must remember. There will come a moment when you're unable to access your notes saved or your calendar, and in those instances you'll be the only thing that is left between you and failing.

Imagine the typical assistant that we all use on our smartphones. You make a list of things to do to make sure you don't remember. You remember the task around an entire week later, and go through your list of tasks. Your digital assistant hasn't reminded your of any task! This is a tech error. Humans, when we've enhanced in our ability to remember, we will no longer be relying on apps that don't work each and every time.

Solutions to Probleme

Solving problems becomes easier when the initial parts of the puzzle are logical. The world is connected and it's our responsibility to us to understand how something affects the other. People who are able to see the connections and keep them in mind when they're needed are the ones to solve the problems and alter the world.

Cognitive Development

Apart from SCHOOLWORK or LECTURES The ability to remember more information can have a positive effect on your brain. How smart can you become? With a strong memory, you'll be able to solve questions and analyse situations with precision and speed.

If your brain can keep track of information and makes you more intelligent in every aspect. It is possible to make your argument, and then defend it since you have a good memory of relevant information. This way, you won't be "arguing without thinking."

The Brain is challenged

Giving your brain a few routine tasks to help it test it. With a stronger memory, you'll be able to think more effectively. As we get older, the more we work out our brains more, the longer we're alert. Training the brain's memory muscles is the best method to slow the natural decline of the brain and remain alert in those years when you'll need it most.

Agile Brain

Your BRAIN is activated when your memory is in good condition. Neurologists believe that recollecting many older facts can make your brain more responsive. This is referred to as "mental gymnastics." It's like that your brain has a flexible structure and able to perform all of the neuro-muscular feats similar to gymnasts.

The ability to retain information is what allows your brain to adapt to working in a healthy manner. Once it is a habit your brain can help you in a variety of situations. In the National Institute of Health and Aging has numerous reports on memory research. The research found that people who have had some form of memory training have brains that are more active than those who did not. After about five years their brain activity continued to be active.

Being a person who has a higher memory is great for any reason you can imagine. There are so many aspects of your daily life in which require your memory. With a clear memory it is possible to perform better learn better, do your studies more efficiently, and rest better. Examine the advantages that an improved memory brings. Choose if you'd like to go through the steps to improve your brain's performance.

What are the reasons you want to improve Your Memory?

Before we can make the most significant growth and the biggest changes, we must get to the point where there is the point of no return. This is the reason why we have programs such as AA and AA. People aren't drawn to them because they feel like they're at the top all the time. People are a part of AA when they hit the bottom of their lane and it's only when they are at their lowest that they can find the courage and strength to make a change in their lives. It is evident that strength can come from a place of negativity, yet produces positive outcomes.

Let's think about the reasons we would like to boost our memory in similar ways. What have you lost because of your poor memory? What number of memories of unforgettable moments with your kids have been lost because you're not sure of how to best store that memory in your brain? What details from the first time you kissed your spouse or the last moment with a loved one are lost to inaccessibility of our brains? Any time you had a chance to remember something, or a moment that went by your way because you didn't remember, that's the motivation, and that's your reason!

If your motivation WHY is greater than your fears of making a complete commitment to improving This is when you're willing to improve...

Imagine your possibilities at work by recollecting the names of those whom you meet. Imagine entering the room of people you've not met since the last trade show and greeting everyone by name. You think it could leave an impression? What if you were able to save and preserve important details regarding watching your son play his first ball in a little league? Imagine the joy that it would keep the memories you cherish in old years. What is it if you're on the edge of another fight with your wife instead of fighting remember with pinpoint precision the time you first met, and then remind her of that moment? Do you think she'll be tempted to throw that cooking pan at you and then?

It's easy to be dismissive of the wonderful things that we can gain from having a strong memory, however, the outcomes are actually real. We know it will help us avoid the unforeseen negative consequences that arise from inadequate memory. We can also imagine what benefits a better memory could hold for us. Make the choice to take on a new path and not stop until you have improved your memory!

For any major change In any drastic change, the most important thing is to determine the reason you wish to make improvements. The HOW is just part of the equation. It's the WHY that's required to determine the best solution.

Before we can learn the exact way experts recall in Part Two ensure that you know why making changes is crucial to your daily life. If you aren't able to be a different you, it's difficult to concentrate and push to make improvements. Take a moment to take this action before moving ahead.

Chapter 7: Filling Your Face With Food For The Best Memory

"If we all were able to appreciate food, cheer and music over gold hoarded in a vault It could be a happier world."

-- J.R.R. Tolkien

D

Did you know that the foods you consume can aid in helping your brain gain clarity, focus and better memory? By incorporating the basic ingredients in our diets is a simple method of building your memory muscle. Because a lot of the work to improve your memory involves mental strain it's nice to know that some tasks require almost no effort.

Below is the list of best food items for memory.

I'll remind you that That I'm not a physician and recommend that you seek the advice of a licensed physician prior to making any diet or medical modifications.

* FATTY FISH - Seafood such as salmon and trout can be fantastic memory enhancers. The reason for this is that our brains are comprised from fat tissue, and a large part of that tissue is Omega-3. Omega-3's are found in the majority of the seafood we consume and is one of the primary building components of our brains. Based on Martha Clare Morris, who examined the effects of fish consumption on brain health, they think that omega-3 in fish that is fatty can help fight Alzheimer's disease.

"* COFFEE-I'm sure I heard a raucous exhale of relief upon hearing the idea of coffee's ability to improve memory. A lot of us begin our day with a cup of coffee, which is why it's the blend of antioxidants and caffeine which seem to aid the brain most. According To the research of Dr.

Astrid Nehlig, coffee has beneficial effects on certain neurological conditions.

* Blueberries - COME ON! it's not much more simple than this. Simply put a few blueberries into your mouth and take pleasure in the antioxidant, anti-inflammatory, the memory-boosting goodness that nature's fruit provides.

* TURMERIC - One the active ingredient found in turmeric is called curcumin. Like blueberries, it's powerful antioxidant and anti-inflammatory. Healthline.com mentions that it's an antidepressant.

* BROCCOLI - This delicious green vegetable is rich in vitamin K. It aids the brain and contributes to better memory. Alongside vitamin K, as well as a host of other beneficial vitamins, it is also a good source of antioxidants.

*PUMPKIN SEEDS - Have you ever eaten baked pumpkin seeds in the fall while carving pumpkins? When I was a kid I did and I didn't think that was the reason I'll never forget the embarrassing incidents I had to endure in my younger years. As with other items in this article, the pumpkin seeds are powerful antioxidants. Additionally, they have significant iron, magnesium copper, zinc, and magnesium.

*CHOCOLATE-GOT Your attention Didn't I? It's precisely dark chocolate that helps improve memory. However, between me and you I'm sure that any chocolate contains brain-boosting chemicals somewhere also, don't you think? When you read the ingredients in the dark chocolate bar when you read with 65% cacao, all it means is that about 65% of the weight's made up of the cocoa bean (cocoa chocolate and cocoa oil too are included). %)--basically the higher the chocolate content, the better percentage. You can trust me, I was in the chocolate-loving town located in Hershey, PA, for most all of my adult life!

* Nuts - These have the dual benefit of strengthening both your heart as well as your brain. Nuts are packed with nutritious fats, vitamins and antioxidants.

* ORANGES - I'M certain you've heard that oranges are packed with vitamin C but do you understand why this is so important? Because, in addition to its numerous advantages, vitamin C helps protect your brain from degeneration when you age.

* EGGS - - According to HEALTHLINE.COM, "Eggs are a abundant source of several B vitamins as well as choline that are essential for development and functioning of the brain and for controlling mood."

*TEA - No this isn't that Iced tea that you can find in the fuel station near the milk.

Real teas, such as rosemary, green Ginkgo biloba, ginseng and peppermint among others can be used to help you fight for better memory and brain health.

Whole grain The final item on the list is whole grains. Since it's a high vitamin E source, all grains should be a part of an appropriate diet plan to keep you alert for the rest of your time.

This isn't a complete list of food items that can aid in improving your cognitive skills and brain function, but eating these foods will certainly help you move towards the correct direction. There are many foods to give you some edge, but in the event that you're receiving sufficient antioxidants and vitamins (B C, D K, B) as well as zinc, magnesium and omega-3 to mention some that will be fine.

There is a reason that not all food choices are all created equal and there are certain foods that you should avoid you want to maintain your mind in good form. These are not only detrimental to your mind as well, they can be harmful to your body too.

* SUGAR - This includes the sweets that you like to enjoy, as well as beverages that are sugary. Sodas, juices and sugary sports drinks result in your blood sugar and insulin levels increase and impair brain function.

* REFINED CARBS and processed Foods in the 1970s, before action movies and the political machinations, Arnold Schwarzenegger was just a freaking powerful dude. The first world-renowned bodybuilder. And when it came to one food group that he was not a fan of the most, it was refined carbohydrates. He used to refer to the refined carbohydrates in the form of "White death." What was he referring to by this? In essence, all white things (white rice and white bread, as well

as white pasta, white flour along with sugar that is white) is something that you must avoid if you want to be at your best. It's true that all old things are newly invented and we're more conscious than ever before that processed foods can be harmful to our well-being. The less chemical and more natural foods you consume, the healthier. These refined carbs aren't doing anything to improve your brain's health and, consequently, will not help your memory. So "steer clear!"

* fake sugar - If it's created in a lab , and there's no need to add it to your body, then I would not. Also, fake soda tastes disgusting, so consume water.

* ALCOHOLIC I know this one also breaks my heart and is likely the main reason I'm not listed on the New York Times Bestseller list. In a serious way I'm pretty sure that everyone doesn't think drinking alcohol can do anything to improve their

health however, you cannot claim that I didn't warn you.

Go to One More Beverage Please!

It's not easy for everyone to grasp that, but the fact is that what you put into your body can make a an impact on how you function, but most importantly the way your memory functions. The brain uses more than a fifth of your body's energy, therefore a balanced diet can result in optimal performance. If you're committed to improving your mental retention, your diet should not be treated lightly. It is essential to ensure that your brain functions at its peak by giving it with the right nutrients.

Habits are important

"Your beliefs are your thoughts."

Your thoughts turn into words,

Your words translate into your actions,

Your actions form your habits

Your actions transform into your values

Your values become your destiny."

-- Gandhi

S

If you've reached this point you've made a commitment to changing your brain regardless of how difficult it may initially appear. We also spent some time looking at what is and isn't included in a diet that boosts brain power. We're still in the initial stage of improvement in memory. This chapter will focus on our daily habits and how they affect our memory.

Once we master the ability to control these daily behaviors, we'll be prepared to master the most fundamental strategies for improving memory. Exciting, right? We're not even into the heart of this book yet, but it's already clear that you have greater understanding of the steps to attain an elite memory level that surpasses 95percent of the population.

Now I'm not going to ask you to modify all of the habits you have in your life, but only one or two. Rearranging our habits is a simple way to prepare our bodies for the changes to take place.

Do not: Multitask

The very first thing we've got in our lives is the notion that multitasking is effective. It isn't, you are sure it's not true, and many research studies have shown it's not true however, why do we continue to do it? My belief is that it's an opportunity to calm our mind.

If you don't devote all your attention on the task in being completed, won't it feel less stressful? If we put in a bit of energy here or a little bit of effort elsewhere We don't have to force us to be focused and focus on a single task. I've experienced this when I try to multitask, I go at a half-speed and achieve only a third of what I need to. Humans aren't designed for multitasking efficiently.

Instead of tricking your mind into believing you're some multitasking superhero, focus on the task in you. You've already discovered that mastery of memory is the stimulation of many senses at once. If you have learned nothing else within this guide, I'd suggest that you get rid of the concept of multitasking from your life.

Do: Engage Your Senses for The Purpose

Let's go back to the possible memory of our son's first baseball game. When you're playing a baseball game, most of the time you're likely to be responding to emails, texting or playing Tetris on your smartphone you think? Sure, I do these things even when I'm just five rows away from the home plate during the Yankees game. It's human behavior. However, the difference is that I don't have to think about the moment. I'm not even a fan Yankees and baseball can become boring! It is important to keep a record of your son's baseball game and keep the memory alive, or you'll regret it. Here's how:

* LOOK - DO NOT take eye contact with the ball for five minutes. Take note of every aspect including dust on your uniform the grass's color and the faded signs on the field, and the right fielder's nose. Consider this as an eye-candy and you're making an image from this particular moment.

* Touch - STAY STILL just for a second. Don't move or fidget with your body in any way. Once you've slowed down the body's movement then slowly start to activate you in the Haptic memory. Make contact with the bleachers that you are lying on or feel the denim fibers in your jeans. Whatever you decide to do, you must stick to the particular movement. One specific

type of finger will help us to carry this moment into the future.

* SMELL JORDAN GAINES LEWIS wrote an interesting piece published in Psychology Today about how smell affects our ability to retain. She wrote, "Incoming smells are first processed by the olfactory that begins in the nose and continues to the lower part of our brain. The olfactory bulb is directly connected to two brain regions that are incredibly involved in memory and emotion the amygdala and the hippocampus. It is interesting to note that auditory, visual (sound) and sensory (touch) information does not travel through these brain regions. This could be the reason why the sense of olfaction (smell) more than all other senses is the most effective at activating memories and emotions."

Therefore, memory is often influenced by what we are able to smell. Even to this day I can smell fresh baked bread and be transported back to my grandmother's kitchen. As I'm sure that you've had the pleasure of experiencing in your own daily life, the smell of freshly baked bread is among the best methods to evoke a memories.

It is possible to use this to our advantage when trying to remember this minor game played in the league. Take several deep breaths, and try to feel the fresh cut grass and halftime bowl of orange slices. If you are able to manage it without appearing like a weirdo, sniff the leather on the glove your son is wearing when you walk back towards the vehicle. Anyone who's played baseball has realized that there isn't any other smell quite as strong.

*TASTE - This is one of the toughest sensory systems to engage in any sense. Similar to smell, taste may provide clues to memories. However, we can only taste a limited amount of things. One way to make use of this in your favor is to chew or eat something that is not familiar during the encode. You can then do the same chewing or eating to retrieve the memory. The next time you study on an exam put an odd-flavored chewing gum in your mouth. You can then chew the same flavor throughout the actual exam.

* SOUND * SOUND SCIENCE has not been confirmed my belief However, luckily for you I'll continue to present the subject and let you make your own decision. It isn't yet clear that music can help you remember, however, we do know that it can do certain things that can aid. First, music can alter our mood. So, when you choose to wear music that soothes you and makes you feel happy You may be more open to new stimuli that trigger memories. Our brains are wired in a way that we may use the left or right side more based on the level of cognition needed for the task. If we are listening to music it is possible to stimulate the brain's two sides. This is my belief however, until I'm proven wrong I think that the more brain's cortex is active during a memory, the more easy it is to recall the memory later on.

During your BASEBALL GAME you could be focused upon the sound that the ball makes striking the glove of the catcher. Perhaps you could better keep the sound from a bat made of wood hitting the left field. In any case you must pay attention to sound of the surrounding area, especially those that are specific to the situation.

Engaging our senses is only one method we can employ to improve the retention of our memories. It's a routine that requires effort but becomes more natural after repeated repetition.

Do: Thank Yourself When You Recall

We often blame ourselves whenever we fail and forget to be happy when we do succeed. Be sure to notice when you are successful and then reframe your thoughts. Make sure you don't allow yourself to be disappointed with the way you performed or did not achieve and cherish the moments when you were proud of yourself. Every night, take time to think about the numerous successes you had in the past day. In many cases, without review, these wins are swept under the rug and forgotten.

Do: Remind Why This Is Important

Every now and then from time to time, it's essential to reflect on what this means for our lives. You should remind yourself why you eagerly want to boost your memory. Be determined to learn and eager about progress. Keep yourself motivated and strive to be a little better every day. In time, these tiny daily gains will turn into major personal successes.

Don't worry, be happy.

As the saying goes, "Don't Worry, Be Happily." When we are relaxed and relax, we're the most relaxed and open to the world around us. Stressing takes effort and energy within your head. Instead of stressing over things you don't manage Try to find meaningful times throughout the day each week, month, and day in which you can recharge and recharge. A calm mind is a great tool.

Do: Always Be Present

This is a habit I have the greatest difficulty with and yet it is the one I find most important. For many people, including myself, it's an everyday struggle to remain in the present moment and not focus on the past or fret regarding the future. Being present naturally makes us reframe our thoughts to see what we're not seeing. It allows us to activate more of our senses, without effort and in general can make us more content.

Living in the present allows the opportunity to reflect and create memories instead of regrets. If you're always focused on the future you're missing out the present! When you are looking to focus and think about the future, do it with purpose. Don't let yourself be distracted by the busy moments all around you to be worried about the next thing that's to come. Also, don't spend your time contemplating the good memories of the past, only to not be able to see the stunning beauty that is right in front of your eyes. There's always another opportunity to think about or reflect and reminisce, but you'll never be able to go back. Always make yourself available.

Do: Exercise

Everyone is aware that exercising is beneficial So I won't dwell on this issue. To boost memory and brain health exercising can do certain aspects that anyone can see an enormous benefit from. It increases the amount of the amount of oxygen that enters the brain, which allows the brain to function at a high level. Additionally, it decreases the risk of developing multiple dementia-related disorders and diseases. The exercise routine causes the body to release positive chemicals such as endorphins and dopamine to the brain. These are the chemicals that make you feel good that cause us to feel as if floating on cloud and improve our mood overall. However, this isn't all. Exercise can also help your brain eliminate the stress-related chemicals and anxiety.

So I know that exercising isn't something you want me to mention for some individuals, but for the benefit of your brain health It's probably the right time to get off the couch. If you're new to exercising, talk to your physician, and begin with a small amount. Sometimes, just one short walk can be enough to create a dramatic change to your body and mind.

There you have it All the habits that develop and then break. Start today and do not waste time. Being aware of the things we're performing and not doing is a significant. Simple changes to your daily routine can have a significant impact on your thoughts. Make sure to focus on small changes and daily moments. Do not be a victim of the failures, instead focus on the successes. It will take many years of work to improve your routines, however the end result is well worth it. It's possible simply by believing that you are able to.

Introduction to Mnemonics

"Every man's memories are his personal literature."

-" Aldous Huxley

S

Before we get to more advanced techniques for memory we'll review some simple memory strategies that have proved effective over generations. The use of mnemonic devices is still effective in our day and age to help recall things. The only requirement is that you must create them by yourself or create them on your own. There's a chance that someone else is the one who created it, but you'll adjust to it to make it easier to remember.

These devices could be used as rhymes, rhymes or even songs. They all relate to the information you need to keep in mind. You can create a memorable acronym that you can remember quickly. You could also utilize the tune of your favourite song to track all the details you require.

Different types of Mnemonic devices

MNEMONIC DEVICES are a simple method to get that memory stuck in your brain for a considerable amount of duration. Other Mnemonic devices include music, visualization as well as the method of loci (method for loci) and so on. They are as follows:

Acronyms

ACRONYMS as well as Weird Expressions

ACRONYMS are another excellent way to keep in mind simple or complex pieces of information. If you want to be able to recall some important detail and then recall it with great accuracy Try this method. One technique I employ is to note every detail I want to recall on flashcards using an image of the word, and the initial letters of the word, on the reverse side. Then, I lay them out in order, and then create the most bizarre phrase I can think of, by writing a phrase which uses the letters in each of the cards. After I'm finished I go through the front and back of the card together a few times, and then arrange them in order to record it in my mind. A good example of this mnemonic device working could be the SWOT analysis, or the standard method of learning the colors that make up the rainbow. It works by combining the initial letters of each item will form a distinctive.

EXAMPLE 1

An example is the SWOT analysis that is used in business circles to assist employees and employers quickly. SWOT stands for Strengths Opportunities, Weaknesses and threats (SWOT). The SWOT is believed to be the work of Albert Humphrey, who created this acronym to highlight the elements that must be remembered, and the significance to each term. Strengths and weaknesses are the first words in the acronym since they're internal variables. While 'opportunities' as well as threats come in second place because they're external variables. This makes them easy to analyze and identify whenever you attend an event. It is unlikely that the person will be in a hurry if asked concerning this SWOT analysis.

EXAMPLE 2

Another EXAMPLE is the world of academia. We all have memories of that 4th-grade Visual Arts topic, "Colors of the Rainbow." Teachers utilized a memory device that was used across the world, and it could also be an acronym. The acronym used to be "ROYGBIV" (Red orange Yellow, Green, Indigo, Blue, Violet). The mnemonic device was influenced from Sir Isaac Newton's famous light experiments "Roy G. Biv." It's a good fit into the pattern of the rainbow colors. Based on this it was incorporated to the Color Wheel of Visual Arts Education.

Visualization

Every visual thing is always notable. This isn't an exaggeration. Many studies have demonstrated the fact that information in visual form is most easy to remember. When it's paired with audio content, it gets better. Our brain enjoys visuals. It is accustomed to the ability to recognize words and sounds as we review and view images.

In a mnemonic tool, we are able to record details in our minds and make mental images - the more bizarre and memorable the more memorable.

Music

Do you remember when you learned to write the alphabet? Most likely not, since it was a long time ago. However, I'd bet that when you begin at A finish at Z most likely, you'll transform into a song before you're done. Music was a key component for learning at an early age and how the alphabet was taught in the schools over the past 100 years. But, the fact that you're no longer a kid does not mean that putting crucial memories in songs will not aid in recollecting them.

The next time you've got crucial facts, figures or dates you'll need to remember you might consider making them into music. We've already discussed how music stimulates different parts of our brains. It can aid us in coding and then retrieve the information.

Rhyming

SIMILAR to music and equally efficient are rhymes. Even to this day, when I think about the months in which I live I'll make rhymes in my head. At school, we learned rhymes for states, presidents and capitals to great effects. There will be more tools for remembering in the future however, for basic recall, there's nothing any easier than making rhymes.

Hook Memory System

This method makes use of the use of numbers as well as mental items to create memories and help keep the information current. This method is best suited when there is a small number of items that must be remembered. For this method to be used begin by making an appropriate hook structure. For this you'll need to number 1-10. Then for each number, choose one that is a rhyme with the number. One example could be: one is Ton (a one-ton weight) 2 = P.U. (something smells) Three is Ski. Following that, you must to construct a vivid image of these images as exact as is possible. In the case of Three = Ski I'd like to color the skis as well as the designs that are on them. Indeed, I could even imagine a skier sporting these skis.

And then, repeat your numbers several times loudly while visualizing the vibrant image. Then, you can picture anything you'll need to recall interacting with these images in the correct order. For instance, if you remember to buy bananas, baked beans and orange juice from the supermarket You could apply this technique.

I'd like to picture a huge baking beans can on the scale that weighs over a ton. There's a heap of smelly brown bananas that have flying flies. Then, a bottle of OJ performing the black diamonds of ski jumping on the snow. You can keep as many things as you can in numerical order by creating the images you imagine in your mind.

This is one of my least favourite ways to keep track of something, but it works for certain people. I'd like to suggest you investigate this method if it appears to be something that could be beneficial for you.

Chunking

There's a saying that goes, "if you want it to be large, begin with a small." When using this device for mnemonics, you have to reduce a huge chunk of information into smaller pieces. This is to help you understand and comprehend the message more easily. It's similar to reading a manual to "how to clean your vehicle." It's not necessary to remember all the details that was written if it was lengthy and long. But if you break it down into chunks it into steps and follow a step-by-step process, the directions are easily remembered.

Another excellent example of chunking could be one of U.S. phone number. It is the U.S. phone number comprises 10 numbers, which are designed to chunk. You shouldn't remember the number by writing it as XXXXXXXXXXX. Learn this number using three different sets of

XXXXXXXXXXX. In actual fact the phone number system that is used throughout the U.S. was specifically designed to make it simpler to remember.

Which MNEMONIC device do you enjoy the most? Find out which method you're most comfortable with so that you'll be able overcome your memory issues.

Basic Tips to Improve Memory

Your brain is wild and unpredictable. We must be as well. If you are trying to remember something whether it's the name, number or location or something else, you need to make it seem strange to your brain. Let's say I have to recall the number 1,475. To firmly fix it in my head I'd imagine the number as a huge fleshy statue, and then imagine snakes slithering through the numbers, and then eating it up, so it was covered in purple blood of an alien! Make it a little bizarre and you'll increase your chances of recalling what you need to.

* I used to better remember names by linking the sound of a name to an image. For instance, if I encountered the name of Brock I could imagine an enormous rock that was perched on the edge of an high cliff. It also works in situations where you are able to relate the name with someone else who has similar name, who is famous or someone you are familiar with. If I encounter a man who is named Victor I'd picture Victor Frankenstein and then of course I'd imagine the huge ugly monster, and boom, I'll forever remember my acquaintance Victor never to forget him!

* CONTINUE to ENGAGE your senses as you're trying to recall. And, again, with Victor I can think of the sound ARRRHHHH Frankenstein produces and the pungent odor of a creature that is made of parts from dead body parts. Whatever senses you're trying to stimulate, allow your mind time to think about the scene and "feel" that sensation. Initially, you'll be slow and the process of memory may feel a bit laborious however, as you continue to work it will become quicker and more efficient.

Write it down! If you're trying to remember something, make a note on paper. Do not type it into your computer because the pen and paper that aids the mind to remember things more effectively.

Create A mind map to help you organize your thoughts. This is the place where your principal idea can be split into multiple parts of a web that connect with similar thoughts. This is what I do when I write the book. I imagine what the main theme is in my mind and the chapters are connected in bubbles that I imagine as if I had written them on a whiteboard.

Re-examine the items you would like to recall. If we don't strengthen what we want to recall, our mind naturally suffers from exponential loss of memory. While we won't totally forget what we're trying to recall However, the proportion of information that we retain is likely to decrease slowly. One method to counter this is to go back and review what you've learned. Start by reviewing each day. If you find that the information is retaining and you want to spread the review further away. It is important to keep track of the extent to which you can remember the information you require and then reducing the duration between review sessions in case you realize that you're forgetting specifics easily.

Teaching someone is the best way to engage new brain regions and increase retention. If you're looking to retain something specific Try explaining the topic to a friend or your spouse like you were teaching. This will make you arrange your thoughts, and sometimes the simple act of organizing the thoughts in our minds protects our minds from being distracted.

These are only a few easy methods to keep in mind that could or might not be suitable for you. Test them out and see what methods work for you, and which don't like at all. Every person is unique and our minds are each different. There is no proper or incorrect method to remember So don't let yourself get discouraged, and continue to work. In the next chapter, we're going to be learning more advanced techniques for memory.

Chapter 8: The Memory Palace

"Time's the murderer of memory"

-" Stephen King, The Gunslinger

M

Do you think this is the most powerful memory strategy ever devised. It is an ancient Greek/Roman memory strategy that's been utilized by chess grandmasters as well as memory champions. It's time to study "The Memory Palace" and once you understand how to build the "palace," it will enable you to keep an infinite amount of information.

A MEMORY PALACE can also be called "the method of loci," in which "Loci" refers to Latin meaning "locations." This is an approach used to remember information that an individual has stored in a computer. Memory Palace Memory Palace is a mental place where you can store images with the mnemonic device. We have discussed before the concept of mnemonic devices, these are methods that you employ to help remember simple as well as complex information.

When you create a memory palace When you create a memory palace, you take an adventure to a location you've been to. There's a specific sequence your journey will follow. Through the sequence that you're capable of creating your dream castle.

The MEMORY PALACE lets you determine how effective you are at recollecting people as well as places, entities, and places. It's not a palace in physical form but it's a location inside your brain, where you keep things in your memories. In addition, it's not so different from the memory you have. However, it's a completely different idea and implies that you'd like to store those memories. You build an Memory Palace based on places or objects that you are familiar with.

The history in the Memory Palace

We can trace the existence in the palace of memory in the beginning of Greek history. The people had to have methods that could be used to preserve information. Writing materials weren't as common to have access to as they are now.

Although the GREEKS developed their memory palace, the idea quickly was used all over the world and was found by Romans. Through his rhetoric Cicero discussed the method. The title for the style was "De Oratore." Cicero explained that the Memory Palace came from Simonides the Greek poet.

Simonides's use in the palace of memory resulted from an event that occurred in his life. Simonides was asked to read the poem at dinner for the higher-class individuals in the society. After reciting the poem Simonides left the banquet before the event was finished. Unfortunately, shortly after his departure the venue fell apart, killing everyone who was inside.

The COLLAPSE was so devastating that no one could recognize the dead in the rubble. The only one who could determine the deceased was Simonides. Simonides remembered where every person who was in the hall, while reciting. He also noted where they were sitting and then, when he walked back to the seat was sitting in it was possible to begin spotting them. This is why, after this experience, Simonides created the Memory Palace method, because it did the trick! (Bower 1970)

In ROME The memory palace was very popular in Rome. This was because of the amazing results its methods brought to people. The success and use of its techniques in the early Roman empire has influenced numerous generations. This is why it has gained use even in more recent times.

DOMINIC O'BRIEN is an eight-time world champion in memory, renowned for his ability to memorize fifty-four decks cards in order, which is 2800 cards. He was able to memorize it by watching every single card and the way they were placed within the deck. Thomas Harris, a novelist is also a fan of his Memory Palace in his novel, Hannibal. The main character, Hannibal Lecter, uses the Memory Palace to locate patient documents. The goal of Hannibal Lecter was to locate individuals to murder.

How does Memory Palace Work? Memory Palace Work?

The first thing to do when creating the Memory Palace is to concentrate. If you aren't focusing and no focus, you don't have a Memory Palace. Another thing you should be aware of is that it is not a good idea to be afraid to concentrate. It might seem like too much work but it's a great way to train your brain to make the memory castle.

It's the Ultimate Mnemonic Device

This METHOD can be beneficial in your home or office, school or car, or any other thing you're familiar with. If you can use your brain to put objects in familiar places, you'll be able to be able to recall these locations. Some even construct the palace of their dreams within their minds However, the trick is creating so vividly that you're able to be intimately acquainted with the area.

How to become a good Memory Palace Creator by Using Other Methods

In addition to MNEMONIC devices There are many other methods that you can employ to become an Memory Palace creator. A lot of these methods are easy to understand and are logical when you consider the ways they can be applied to memory.

You can have a technology recess

Yes, it is possible to you should take a break from technology reminders. Your brain might even function more efficiently than technology. For instance, you may have an app on your smartphone for reminders of the things that you frequently forget. You may have scheduled an activity to a certain date and time. However, if you're able to recall that time two hours prior you'll be more productive than a assistant. We never know what's going take place in the next moment. I'm sure that everyone has had to deal with power outages or the phone not working while you're waiting for the alarm to get you up to go to work. It can happen if you depend on technology to compensate for a lack of memory. It will eventually fail you and this could happen at the worst moment.

It's better to take care in order to have an amazing memory.

The digital assistant you receive doesn't really help your brain. It's just there to assist you to complete the next task you're scheduled to do and that's it. You are dependent on this aid that you're memory doesn't get affected any longer. When you're working to activate your brain, put your computer or phone off (except in the event that you're required to use it to work). This will help you focus on your brain , not the other elements surrounding you.

BE Intentionally

If you need to remember an event or person has passed away, there is an incentive to do it. If you truly desire to recall something, speak about it with your self and thinkto yourself "I need to keep this in mind. I don't want to be forgotten". Sometimes, uttering words to yourself will yield positive outcomes. It's because you've set your intention to achieve it.

After meeting a new person Try making use of a device recall. For example you meet a new person at your school of music has the name "Samantha." It is possible to be reminded of the famous singer Sam Smith. "Sam" with"sam" with a "th" is Samantha. It's hard to remember names however, when you require the name of a person it's time to make it happen! Create a memorable sounding name or include more details than the name. This was a technique that former President George W. Bush used to recall names. It was used in the film W. by actor Josh Brolin.

If you've been to an area, you should create the reason why you must remember the place. Make use of mnemonic devices to help you remember the name so that you are able to remember it in the future. The reason might not be true however, you're making use of it to help develop your brain's capacity to better remember information. You must challenge your mind to never forget this information each moment you write it down.

Becoming interested

You're trying to develop better memory, aren't you? Why not try as many times as you can be attracted? Being interested in a particular fact or idea can help you focus and recall quickly. In some cases, you don't require an memory aid. Your knowledge of the subject will cover any distraction that could make you forget.

Be aware that "this is an important topic." It could appear like you don't need it everywhere you travel. However, in the end there's a chance that a discussion about it may spark. You'll be able contribute to the conversation based on the information you've gathered from yourself.

Here's a prime example. Imagine you're watching a documentary on solar power in a different part in the globe. If your home does not use solar power then you might not be interested in recollecting the most important facts. If you are able to alter your mindset it can make nearly everything more fascinating. You decide instead to take an interest because in the near future, policies could be changed. Perhaps, in the future, renewable technology could become something that grants you the tax benefits and also can save you money. Look for ways that makes things more interesting and useful to your everyday life. For instance, if you're trying to increase your memory by getting interested in solar power, you'll not consider making use of solar energy. Instead, you'll think to your self, "this is some interesting secure technology. Please let me know how this functions". While watching you watch, you're attentive and are captivated. It might also inspire you to go online to find details on something exciting.

Take notes

THIS is the most popular method of improving memory, also known as 'remembering. If you have to recall an individual, place or item it is best to write the information down. The journal you keep allows you to reference it at any time you require the information.

From time to time from time to time, you'll be able to write your information down on the paper. It is essential to make sure the information doesn't disappear. Also, you shouldn't keep all the information in a notebook. The best option is to put the information in chunks on your notebook or on paper. This will help you make it easier to identify the crucial points you require for the information.

The most important aspect of mastering memory is concentration. It is essential to spend the time to work each detail of your mind and ensure that you are able to visualize your dream palace in a way that is as detailed as a photograph before you. If you can master this skill, you'll be among the elite in the field of memory. The reason this is difficult is due to the beginning difficulty. Once you've got an the right strategy to build your dream home, you'll discover how much simpler it becomes.

Step-by-Step Tutorial on Building Memory Palace Memory Palace

"Memories even your best ones disappear quite quickly. However, I'm not with the idea. The memories that I treasure most, I never think about them disappearing."

-- Kazuo Ishiguro, Never Let Me Go

C

Re-creating the concept of a Memory Palace is imaginary, sure. However, it is a meticulous plan. It is essential to engage your brain to aid in memory to develop successfully. It's an enjoyable process that becomes easier with time. As with all things initially, beginning to try it can be the most difficult, then it becomes much easier. You'll realize that you've had a wonderful time throughout and it's not as hard as you believed it would be.

Six Steps to Building the Memory Palace

1. Choose Your Palace

The place you choose must be one you are familiar with. The objective is to determine how the method will perform. You'll be testing your ability to recognize things in the space you've selected as your personal space. It is important to imagine yourself there, whether it your office or your home. Through this method you're using your eyes'.

For greater effectiveness, make your home your home since it's the first location you're familiar with. If you can visualize your home it will help you train your memory. Make an effort to recall every object in your room and imagine it in your mind. You can remember it in a series or employ the method of location.

If you can remember the order of their appearance or the location they are in This helps improve your memory. Other palaces that you could make use of are the streets and your school, or your workplace or even a nearby park. You must have something you're familiar with and make a vivid picture of within your head.

2. Find Specific Features

Next, you should be aware of the different parts of the palace you have chosen. If you chose your location, the most visible thing you'll notice is the trash can on the end that runs alongside the street. Take a stroll through the area in your Memory Palace. Imagine someone running by threw an empty bottle into the garbage can near your home. What is the house that is next to the trash can? And, what are the color? If trees are found outside the home, which residence is it? Discover the thing that draws you in, something you'll never forget. When you are reminiscing about all of these things, make notes of them. Divide these notes so it is possible to fill these up with the details you'd like to keep in your mind.

3. Plan the Route

This is a crucial step. In order to create an enchanting memory palace You must plan out a plan. For instance, you're using your school. There are a variety of routes which will take you to various classes. Also, when you enter the home you might visit the bedroom of your brother prior to going into your own. Be congruous with your path and keep it within your mind's palace. Pick the route you like to make it more convenient for you. If the school you attend is your personal memory apex keep it in your memory. Make sure you walk straight to your class from the front entrance. You may visit the school physically and follow the directions. So, you'll keep track of the route within Your Memory Palace.

I. You could walk from the entrance of the school through the main entrance to the outdoor passageway.

II. Then, go through the main door.

III. Then, the hallway.

IV. You go to the first staircase , and then to the second. After that, you go through three entrances to the right side before reaching the door to your classroom.

You could extend your castle to the seat at the table. Keep in mind that while walking around and memorizing this route, you must have a piece or paper. Write down the most common features of each place. Include visual characteristics such as size, material, color and feel of the surface, design and shape. What scent does it have? The more senses that you can integrate in your mind, the better the memory will be. When you next attempt to go through the palace of your mind it is possible to focus more on the images at this point and not think about anything else. Review your notes and written down the path. Once you're sure you've got your Memory Palace route is set in your head then you're ready to move on to following the steps.

4. Associate

Connect an event you would like to keep in mind. Create a connection between it and the places within Your Memory Palace. You can collect one item at one time to make the process simpler. Then, make an imaginary picture of these objects and let them interact with your place. This is why we'll use to create the Memory Palace in the previous step: your school.

5. Begin to Use Your Mnemonic Devices

You already know your home and the way you'd like to take. You're also aware of the features of this device. Now, you're ready to start using your Mnemonic devices. Make use of rhyme, song or acronym to help you remember the facts.

6. Revisit Your Palace

It's always a good idea to go back and revisit your home. Check everything you've made. Make sure that nothing has changed. However, if there was a change changed something, go to the place and make sure that it is an element to Your Memory Palace.

The MEMORY PLAACE is always a blast. It's exciting for anyone who uses it to enhance memory. It's all you need is hard work to get your mind on a particular job, but it's possible to build a memory that is almost as powerful as. It stretches your brain and helps you prepare for a variety of challenging situations. This helps improve your memory and increase it to the highest range of your brain's capabilities.

The list you make will stay in your mind for several days or even weeks. It is possible to create additional Memory Palaces to store other items you'll want to keep in mind. They can come in a variety of styles, and aren't required to be identical to the first one you built. You can look through the list of mnemonic devices and the various locations you can utilize to create creating your Memory Palace. If you're interested utilize the latest loci, but make sure you understand the new structures of loci before making use of them. Begin by creating and re-creating the scene.

Ideas for Creating the Memory Palace

The process of creating A Memory Palace may seem difficult to you at first. Here are some suggestions that you can adhere to when you are creating the Memory Palace to simplify the process.

Growing LOCI

LOCUS IS A SPECIFIC POINT, POSITION or location. loci is the plural version of it.

When you realize that you've used all of your loci using your other Memory Palaces

Find another. For instance, you could make use of the corner of your bed cabinet as a location. The route will begin at one end of the cabinet, and will end on the other side. Other possible locations be the corner on the left or the left corner, the wall adjacent, the opposite wall as well as the ceiling, the floor, and finally the entryway.

The new location could be a friend's home, or a map of a video game that you're used to. It could be any other route you're familiar with. Your favourite store, personal spa, gym, salon or shopping complex as well as a parks for recreation could be your point of entry.

Keeping Track of Your Memory Palace: Adding Qualities and telling a story

To ensure you keep an eye on the details of Memory Palace, you can note down the entire journey and the various locations you'll be using. It is also possible to utilize the same location at some point. The best thing to do is add more features to this travel.

Another way to keep an eye on the contents of your Memory Palace is to connect things and your travels. In this means you're telling the story of your journey, which provides additional ways to trigger memories. Create an account in Your Memory Palace. It's not just entertaining, but you will be able to see the connection between the items you have in the items in your Memory Palace.

Take note of the fact that if the objects are greater than the loci, you are able to put two or three items within one location. Make sure that the items easily interact with each other in the same locus to make it easy to remember. So, your items aren't just referring to the place and are also pointing to each other. For instance, you could have the Keurig coffee maker as well as the tiny cups that sit inside it. They are both connected, but they're used for different reasons.

So, using Memory Palace Memory Palace, you've told an epic tale that includes an outline (sequential sequence of events) as well as a the setting (your castle and location) as well as the character and action, props and even light (well it's not the case that every location has such a bright, glowing light, but it's one of the distinctive features).

Making Memories in a Short Book an Memory Palace

To memorize a book using the help of your Memory Palace, you must first determine what you would like to remember. What is the story? Section headings? Or, is it the whole text? Whatever way you decide to accomplish it, let's start!

The first thing to build will be the castle. It is important to choose your palace in accordance with the places we've talked about before. If your book contains 10 sections, make sure that your palace contains 10 loci. It could be ten homes in the street, or ten mailboxes on the homes. If you are following these instructions read the instructions for creating an memory palace in the previous book.

The next step is to read each part of the text. After you've finished with one, determine which information you'd like to retain from the section and incorporate it in the palace. Begin your journey by reading the beginning chapter and interact with the initial loci. It's a novel such as. You have to remember every chapter to be able to write an essay. Place the chapters in your home, and allow your castle to be the whole book. The very first chapter might be about a child who was lost on his bicycle the middle of an Haunted House. What you need to do is allow this event to connect with your initial place of reference.

If you are able to move to other chapters, you should follow the same procedure. This way, you're moving the story towards your surroundings. It's like taking the story home and not let it be buried in the novel's setting.

So, if you're reading a self-help guide collect the ideas or lessons from each chapter. It should be linked to your location. Also, if it's a novel a short story, let the major story to connect to the location in every chapter.

Change Your Direction

Your place of work HAS different directions, which means you can alter your course in order to be flexible. For example, your palace is in your house. Your journey began by walking toward the trash can , and then on the right side of the street. The next step could be that you walk far away from the garbage bin. It might begin by taking a walk to the right of your lawn to the house of your neighbor. In this way, you get an alternate view of the palace, with different styles and colors, and numerous objects in the vicinity. This isn't just changing the direction you're looking at and perspective, but also increasing your perspective.

Overcoming Background Problems

It could be problematic when two of your locations share a common background. Also, if your brain uses the background as a way to remember information, that could be a problem. It's best not to focus on the colour on the walls or floor. This way, you will be able to discern between the left wall and the right one, or the floor's remaining corner and the right corner of the floor and vice versa.

A REAL-LIFE EXAMPLE OF the effects of Memory Palaces. Memory Palace

One thing you should know is the Memory Palace is useful if you make a commitment to it. It is also not a thing to relate to your background, age, education and sex, the status of your marriage, or any health medical condition. Anyone can do it. Don't get discouraged when it's difficult at first. As you begin; it will get easier. Start by focusing on small details and then progress to more complicated recall.

In 2010 there was a study conducted in Norway about how effective Memory Palace could be. Memory Palace could be (Engvig and co. 2010). The experts instructed 23 volunteers in how to utilize Memory Palace. Memory Palace technique. They were all the age of 61. Each participant was able to memorize 30 words in the correct sequence in just 10 minutes.

Another group of people of similar age, education background, and sexual orientation were also part of the study. They were not trained in this technique. Memory Palace Technique but were instructed to recall the 30 items.

The researchers asked both groups to go to their normal routines throughout eight weeks. When that time was over they asked the researchers the groups what they had learned two months prior.

The Final Result

After eight weeks The researchers tried something and different this time. They showed 15 unrelated words to the untrained and trained participants. Then, they presented them with 30 words they had never heard of. The majority of the words were original, whereas they had presented the other at first.

They were all told to identify all words from the first 15 minutes and put them in the proper order. The participants who had learned how to use the Memory Palace technique performed better than those who did not. (Engvig et al., 2010).

ALSO they were able to identify the proper positions for every word. They may have used devices for mnemonics to aid in their memory. Based on the study it's evident that Memory Palace technique is effective for both short and long-term memories.

Chapter 9: How Discipline Is The Key To Success

"I believe it's the matter of love. The more you cherish a memory, the more ferocious and strange it becomes"

-- Vladimir Nabokov

T

Here is the only time there was one thing that stood against you from achieving everything that you've always dreamed of. It's discipline. If you thought that I would say something different I'm sorry to disappoint you. To build a strong memory, that you take an organized and disciplined approach. You must spend every day looking for ways to develop and strengthen your brain.

Don't forget that your brain is a muscle similar to your biceps, or your quads. It requires to be worked and stimulated as well as resting repeatedly. The world's top memory athletes did not get their current position in a matter of hours. They worked hard and trained and worked hard to improve their memory, no matter how long or how challenging it was.

I'm guessing that you're not looking to become the next memory guru. It's likely that you want to make improvements in the everyday things that you do, such as recalling a person you've just have met or not forgetting to buy the fruits in the supermarket. It's okay as everyone is unique, and our goals are as diverse as the ones we set for ourselves. However, just because your objectives aren't as big doesn't mean you're free from responsibility. It is still necessary to discover simple methods to improve your brain's performance every day. In order to get the desired results it is essential to be focused. This isn't for the weak of heart or the lazy. You'll need to test your brain every day and, at times, you'll not succeed.

If you do it correctly you may be able to gain more than just an excellent memory. It is possible that with a little training for memory and providing your brain the resources it needs to be at its peak to be able to achieve greater heights in your job, friendships with family and friends, as well as relationships. The right diet and exercise routine can aid in making your brain work harder quicker, more efficiently, and for longer. In fact, if the only thing this book taught you was the skills you required to get faster and more agile with your comingbacks, it was definitely worth the effort. The first step to discipline is to put yourself in the best possible position to succeed, which is why I encourage for you to implement the diet adjustments necessary to improve. Get started exercising, no matter how you aren't able to do it, and then build from there. Be confident in yourself and the person you could become. When everything else is put in order, then it's the time to train, and in the next section, I'll teach you how to get there.

Strategies to Improve Your Memory

"Memory is more permanent as ink."

--- Anita Loos

A

Are you ready to hear an exciting announcement? It's not as difficult as it may appear. There are a few methods of training require lots of focus and effort however, most are simple. I'll begin with a list of techniques which are easy to use and most enjoyable.

Board Games

Yes, sometimes improving your memory and ability to think is as easy as having a weekly game night with buddies. Thinking strategically and making decisions can stimulate different areas of your brain to improve the cognitive abilities. The best part is that when you stay clear of games like Boardwalk as well as Park Place, board games reduce stress and boost happiness. They can also increase patience and enhance short and long-term goals.

Jigsaw Puzzles

Like board games Puzzles are a great option to stay focused and boost memory. The simple nature of a jigsaw puzzle allows for effortless memory improvement since it forces users to utilize spatial memory. Spatial memory can be classified into short and long-term memory . It lets you remember the different places of objects as well as the "spatial" distance from each other.

IMPROVE Vocabulary

Learning and using words that are unfamiliar is a great method to improve your brain. It is possible to purchase an idea for the day planner, and then try to use the word of the day every day. It is possible to boost the idea by making it clear as well as writing it in your notebook several occasions throughout the day. Improve your vocabulary is a straightforward method to improve your intelligence to sound smarter and feel more intelligent.

Engage the senses

Find an activity that will enable you to engage several senses simultaneously. Enjoy an excursion with a companion as you take time to pause and breathe in at the crisp mountain air. Participate in a cooking class and gain a new skill eating, tasting, and cooking. Explore the floral shop and take a moment to take a sniff of the roses. These activities help to stimulate your brain and also allowing you to make exciting dates. If you're similar to me, you'll find that a few of these dates aren't too expensive either.

Listen to music and move your body

Listening in tune while you move stimulates numerous areas in your brain. It is known that music activates both brain regions and dance incorporates our fine motor abilities. But don't worry about it even if your motor skills aren't great when you're around the floor are able to always dance in your living room. It doesn't matter which music you listen to or how you move, simply doing both can provide your brain with a boost in terms of power and creativity thinking. What is an all-in-one threat? Include singing along to the beat when dancing and you'll be an expert in memory and you'll feel like NSync. Incorporate this into your routine and you'll be able say Goodbye, Bye, bye to brain fog for good once and for all.

Change Something

Our brains thrive when we provide it with additional data to analyze. Simple things like taking a stroll with your family along unfamiliar roads or choosing an alternate route to work can provide your brain the needed stimulation. When I get stuck with a problem I will often get myself away from the familiar and explore a new place. A new environment will help you to see issues or solutions new perspective.

Try Yoga

YOGA can give your brain an energy boost as well as helping you get in shape. Because it is a combination of complicated movements, innovative movements as well as meditation and breathing and improves the brain in ways that scientists are yet to fully comprehend. If yoga isn't your style then you may want to consider Tai Chi to help you remain focused and improve your memory and thinking skills.

Discover Something New

NEW stimuli always cause our brains to work harder to comprehend it. So, each when we discover something new, we strengthen our brains. If you can recall earlier in this book we discussed the science curriculum in high school and my experience of how I failed in Chemistry. Of course, this was because I did not have an sources to go to when I was confronted with the brand new materials they required me to master. The more you learn more, the simpler it is for learning later on. This is because it provides you with an excellent foundation to evaluate and compare with the new information you receive in relation to what you've had previously learned or seen.

The same way If you're facing something that is new and you are preparing your brain. This will help you retain much more information than you could have. Here's how:

1. Before you start learning something new, you should make the following list of 5-10 high-level items you are aware of about the area.

2. Then, take the list and under each of the 5-10 items of the top level, write in something you are aware of about each item.

3. In your head, try to trace a line between what you're studying relates to the first-level subjects and to the 2nd level items below it.

4. Once you're done, you've already connected a variety of information within your brain and are ready to discover something different.

Do not use lists.

Next time you visit the supermarket Do not make an inventory. You must force yourself to remember the items on it with some of the memory tools you have learned. If you're not sure you can write an outline and keep it in your purse, however, don't make use of it. It's a way to build your memory just like you are doing bicep curls in the gym. The more you push your brain to fight to remember, the easier it is to recall what you'll need in the near future.

Be Hyper Observant

Next time you're walking around, you should be focusing on the things around you. How do the people dress? What is their style of dress? Pay attention to the surroundings that you're in? What kind of wallpaper do you see on the walls? And what colors are you seeing? You can get yourself out of the comfortable state of blissful ignorance and really pay attention to every aspect of your surroundings. After you have left take the time to recall each and every detail you recollected. Do this every day and it's one of the most simple and most effective ways to improve your memory. Here's a game that I created to test my memory:

1. Choose 10 specific things to recall (color of wallpaper, flooring and the clothing of the individual and facial expression etc.). I use this method when I'm in a shop; it does not work at home or in a location that you're intimately acquainted with.

2. When you are at the moment, pay attention to the particulars and absorb all aspects of them.

3. Once you return to your vehicle, immediately replay the entire experience in your mind. Try to remember the percentage of the details remember. To make it more difficult and memorable I

attempt to keep all of the details in a sequence when I remember it in my brain.

4. Repeat this exercise, and the next time try and remember items 10 min later after 30 minutes and 3 hours later.

Every day, doing this can help you improve your observational skills and improve your memory. It's one of the most simple and most effective methods to improve your memory and monitor the quality of your retain, encode, and recall memories. If you are able to recall the specifics of a trip to the supermarket the following day without difficulty You'll notice that if you are focused on a discussion or presentation you'll be able to recall it later on as well.

Here is a list of some easiest ways to build that brain muscle. There are numerous applications designed to help improve your memory and attention. Certain apps like BrainHQ and Lumosity are enjoyable and meet their promises. I would suggest removing games from your smartphone that don't stimulate your brain, and replacing them with apps that help you think more critically. This way, the next time you're waiting on the train instead of spending time on useless games that don't help you, you're strengthening the most vital muscle.

As You Age

If you are looking through this book and thinking the best way to reduce the decline in your cognitive abilities as you get older I'd recommend you to refer back to this chapter. The information included in this chapter is applicable on you once you grow older. But, it will become less of a recommendation and more of an obligation. Maintaining your senses in top shape by using your senses and learning can increase the stimulation of your brain. The best method to keep your mind in check and maintain your memory as you get older is to simply believe that you are capable. If you didn't believe in stereotypes and limitations that the world imposed on your when you were younger then why should you now believe them? Perhaps you didn't have confidence in yourself and confidence, but you're more mature as you get older. You've been through more and seen more, so you should every day, take time to take a moment to reflect on the person you are and what you can accomplish.

Chapter 10: What Do You Have The Potential To Accomplish?

We've all heard humans' brains are extremely capable, however, the majority of us don't realize the extent that the brain is actually capable of or what it actually accomplish. Your brain is used every day , and you believe you are aware of the capabilities of your brain? In reality, you don't. There are many myths that are believed to be real.

The truth behind the most popular misconceptions about memory and the brain.

* A larger brain won't make you more intelligent. Even Albert Einstein had a relatively small brain!

* You cannot utilize 100% of your brain because you already use it! There's nothing hidden, other potential that you could access. Your brain is in motion every day even when you're not.

* Hypnosis CAN'T retrieve forgotten memories.

* There's not a secret formula to have a great memory.

However, the majority of them were right . You really can do incredible things. Your brain is highly flexible and it can become more efficient through focused training!

The same is true for memory. There isn't a secret formula to develop a great memory but you can jot down the vast majority of data using specialized methods.

To show it, here are a few official records from the World Memory Championship:

* SPEED CARDS Simon Reinhard from Germany managed to retrieve a one 52-card deck with 21.19 seconds.

* SPOKEN NUMBERS - Jonas von Essen from Sweden remembered 380 digits.

* HOUR CARDS Ben Pridmore from Nottinghamshire in the UK is the only person to be credited with recalling 14,556 cards from 28 decks in just one hour.

* BINARY NUMBERS: Ben Pridmore was able to remember 4,140 binary numbers, strings of numbers containing 1 and 0 in just 30 minutes.

* NAMES AND FACES another accomplishment to Simon Reinhard is that he identified and remembered faces and names of 186.

* HOUR NUMBERS Wang Feng from China holds the record for most random numbers, in 40 rows that can be recalled in less than one hour

* RANDOM WORDS : We have another appearance by the german Simon Reinhard who holds the record for the number of random words that can be recorded in 15 minutes.

* HISTORICAL DATES Johannes Mallow holds the title of being able to remember 132 dates and the events they're linked to in just five minutes

* ABSTRACT IMAGES Mallow is also the king of abstract images, having recalling 492 pictures within 15 minutes.

* SPEED NUMBERS Mallow also holds a record-breaking joint record of remembering 501 numbers, arranged in 40 rows in just five minutes

Amazing, right?

And I'm sure I understand the thoughts you're having. I'm here to tell you that these people aren't superhumans They don't have any superpowers. They've just discovered how to utilize memory strategies which are also referred to as Mnemonic devices.

What is a mnemonic device?

Mnemonic devices are a method you can utilize to enhance the ability of you to remember things. Mnemonics aid learners in recalling huge chunks of information such as parts, steps of stages, or phases with 100 percent accuracy.

It's a method of memory to help your brain organize the information, encode it and then recall it. It's a shortcut that lets you connect the information that you'd like to keep in mind using an image sentence or word.

In the current century among the best researched and fascinating memories belongs to Russian journalist as well as professional mnemonist Solomon Shereshevsky. As per the neuropsychologist Alexander Luria, who studied Shereshevsky for over thirty years, there were no limits in his memories. As a journalist Shereshevsky never made notes during his interviews, but his writings were extremely detailed and precise. He explained to his editor that he did not have to keep notes because the journalist never lost anything!

Like many memory magicians, Shereshevsky had his own unique system of mnemonics. Luria realized that shereshevsky was born with the ability of synesthesia which utilized all his senses when recalling things.

If he heard music the notes would trigger flashes of colour. If you touched something that was touched, it made him feel a the sensation of tasting. He could recite the poem in a different language by connecting the words with similar sounds in Russian and English, even though they were different in meaning.

Nowadays, a lot of people are employing these kinds of systems. It's the most effective method of storing details as well as "sticking" it in your brain for easier recall later on.

A study conducted in 1967 conducted by Gerald R. Miller showed that mnemonics can actually increase recall. Miller discovered that students who used regularly Mnemonic devices increased their test scores to 77 percent!

Certain mnemonic devices are from the early Greek times. It is dedicated in this book to one of the more well-known methods of mnemonics, which were used in the earliest Roman and Greek literary treatises: the Memory Palace which is also called the Method of Loci.

Meet The Memory Palace as well as the Method of Loci

The Method of Loci is the oldest mnemonic system known to mankind. It has been utilized from ancient times to learn speeches and other vital information.

The method relies on the idea that you are most likely to recall locations that you are familiar with. All you have to do is connect the details to a location which you're familiar with and it will provide an indicator that can assist you remember.

As per Cicero In the work Rhetorica ad Herenium, the system was invented through the poetry of Simonides of Ceos who was the sole survivor of a collapsed building during an evening meal. Simonides was able to identify all who was missing or dead, by recollecting where guests were in the room.

Memory Palace Memory Palace was used by both Greek and Roman orators who could give speeches without the use of notes.

This method will give you the most effective results if you're skilled in visualizing things.

What is the best way to make use of it?

To apply to use the Method of Loci, you have to connect things that you would like to remember with the locations of a familiar space or building, or even a street. In order to find the details, you just have to stroll through the area and the images will appear in your head instantly.

To be more effective it is necessary to visualize the object performing something in an exact spot.

Let's construct it...

1. Imagine a location you are familiar with.

When you first start I would suggest using the pathway that runs through your home.

2. You must now divide the way to one of the location.

For our first test We will require the following 10 items. Imagine how you usually get to your bedroom when you return home. When you walk into each of the rooms, make sure you move to the right direction from one end in the space to opposite.

Remember that you need to take the exact route around your home each time, or you'll experience a mental block.

Did you finish? Let's go to the gym!

www.ingramcontent.com/pod-product-compliance
Lightning Source LLC
Chambersburg PA
CBHW050406120526
44590CB00015B/1845